Fascinating Facts
About The Human Body

A Science Book

For Grades 4–6

written by Andrew Thompson and Becky Daniel

edited by Lynn Bemer Coble, Carol Rawleigh,
Gina Sutphin, Melinda Lim Taylor, and Kathy Wolf

illustrated by Cathy Spangler Bruce

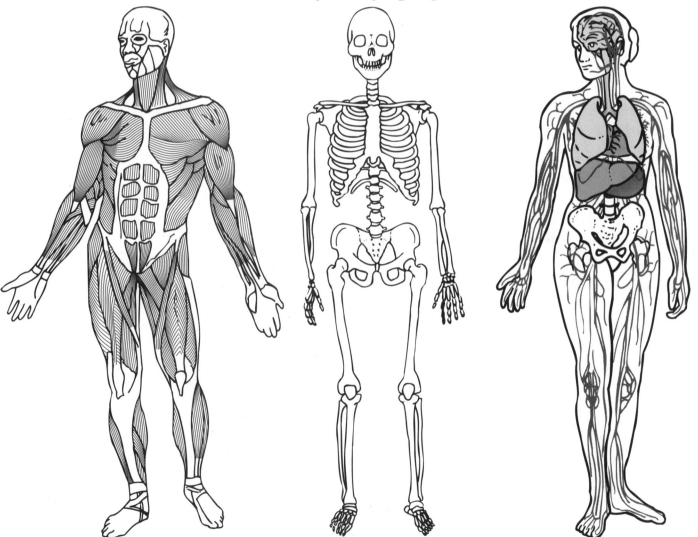

ISBN# 1-56234-114-6

Manufactured in the United States
10 9 8 7 6

To The Teacher

Fascinating Facts About The Human Body is filled with amazing facts guaranteed to astound your students. Do you know that you can't sneeze with your eyes open? Do you know that if your blood vessels were laid end to end, they would stretch around the equator 2 1/2 times? Do you know that your blood cells rush around your body faster than race cars at the Indianapolis 500? Do you know how many pints of blood your body has in it? Do you know you have billions of nerve cells in your brain nourished by a trillion surrounding cells? Your students are sure to be awed by these facts and hundreds of other interesting facts about their miraculous bodies!

The text includes fascinating facts about body systems including the circulatory, lymphatic, respiratory, skeletal, muscular, nervous, sensory, digestive, endocrine, and reproductive systems. Subjects covered are cells, bones, tendons, joints, the brain, the knee, the elbow, the shoulder, arms, legs, the five senses, and dozens of others. Students will enjoy the variety of fun-filled formats used to reinforce the fascinating facts. Crossword puzzles, word searches, diagrams to color, and terms to match make the learning of thousands of facts easy and fun. When children complete this book, they will have a general knowledge of their amazing bodies and how their bodies work.

Each worksheet includes RESEARCH and BONUS questions or activities that will add depth to the classroom learning experience. Many of these activities can be done as a class or be given to a small group or an individual as a special challenge. Award special recognition to those who complete a RESEARCH or BONUS activity. On page 128, there are special gold-medal award certificates for those who complete a given number of these activities.

To culminate this learning unit, there is a human body facts trivia game found on page 103. Use the question cards (pages 104—118) to challenge teams, pairs of students, or individuals. The game cards may also be used as flash cards for review. Award students' hard work with the certificates found on pages 125–128.

Table Of Contents

Introduction

Understanding The Human Body (anatomy and physiology) 5

Looking Through The Microscope (the microscope) 7

Amazing Systems (body systems) 9

Marvels Of Design (cells) 11

Building Blocks (cells) 13

Circulatory System

An Efficient System (circulatory system) 15

Tubes For Carrying Blood (blood vessels) 17

Oxygen And Nutrient Carrier (blood) 19

A Busy Pump (heart) 21

Tiny Tubes (capillaries) 23

Germ Busters (lymphatic system) 25

Shaped Like A Bean (kidneys) 27

Respiratory System

A Breathtaking System (respiratory system) 29

The Nose Knows (nose) 31

Catch Your Breath! (breathing) 33

Skeletal System

Saved By A Skeleton! (bones) 35

Big Bones And Little Bones (bones) 37

Inside Bones (bone marrow) 39

Up And Down Your Spine (vertebrae) 41

The Tailbone (tailbone) 43

Knee Knowledge (knee) 45

The Excellent Elbow (elbow) 47

Shifting The Shoulder (shoulder) 49

The Long Bones (arms and legs) 51

Body Cushions (cartilage) 53

Joining With Joints (joints) 55

Muscular System

Connecting Muscle And Bone (tendons) 57

Every Time You Move (muscles) 59

Nervous And Sensory Systems

The Beautiful Brain (brain) 61

Brainy Bonanza (brain) 63

What's On Top? (head) 65

Spinal Signals (spinal cord) 67

You Get Under My Skin! (skin) 69

The Second Layer (skin) 71

Knowing About Nails (fingernails and toenails) 73

I Only Have Eyes For You! (vision) 75

Now Hear This! (hearing) 77

The Sensing Senses (the five senses) 79

Digestive And Endocrine Systems

Dealing With Digestion (digestive system) 81

Tracking Digestion (digestive system) 83

Chomping And Chewing (teeth) 85

The Hardest Substance (teeth) 87

Ten Thousand Taste Buds (mouth) 89

The Body's Chemical Factory (liver) 91

Sugar Regulator (pancreas) 93

The Interesting Intestines (intestines) 95

The Body's Messengers (body chemicals) 97

Reproductive System

Reproduction And Fertilization (sperm and ovum) 99

Chromosomes And Genes (genetics) 101

The *Fascinating Facts About The Human Body* Game

Fascinating Facts Game Rules 103

Fascinating Facts Game Cards 104

Answer Key 119

Awards 125

Marvels Of Design

Directions: Use the number code to label and color the diagram of a cell.

1. The **nucleolus** is the small mass at the center of a cell. Color it light blue.
2. The **nucleus** surrounds the nucleolus and has strands of chromatin, which make up the chromosomes. Color the nucleus dark blue.
3. The **nuclear membrane** surrounds the nucleus. Color it green.
4. **Cytoplasm** is the jellylike substance that surrounds the nucleus and holds everything else in the cell. Color it pink.
5. The **cell membrane** is the wall that encloses and protects the contents of the cell. It is flexible and can change shape easily. Color it orange.

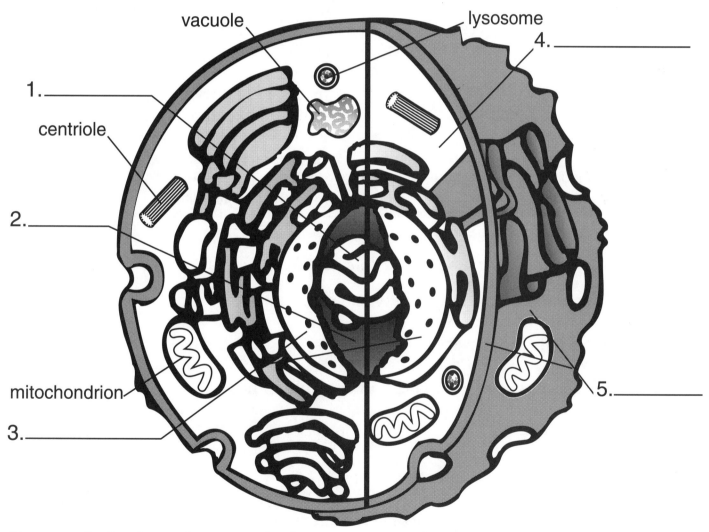

Research: Look up these words: *lysosome, vacuole, mitochondrion,* and *centriole*. After you read about each one, color it on the diagram of the cell.

Bonus: If exactly 1,000,000 old cells die each second, how many die each minute? Each hour? Each day? Each week?

Marvels Of Design

Cells come in all kinds of shapes and sizes. Some are round, some are flat, and some are even square!

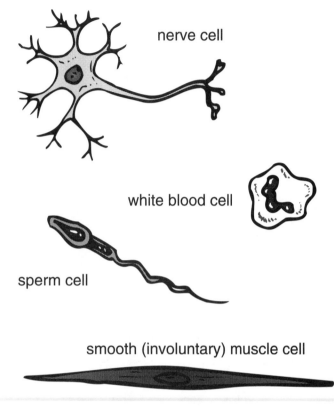

nerve cell

white blood cell

sperm cell

smooth (involuntary) muscle cell

Human bodies are marvels of design. The smallest unit in the body is the cell. An average cell is about 1/1,000 inch across. Can you imagine anything as small as that? Every second, millions of old cells die and millions of new cells replace them.

There are many different kinds of cells. Some of these are red blood cells, fat cells, muscle cells, bone cells, nerve cells, brain cells, and skin cells. From a four-foot-long nerve cell to the smallest sperm cell, each has a different shape and a different job. No cell works alone. Cells work together tirelessly day and night, never stopping, to keep your amazing body working!

Directions: Write T for true or F for false before each statement.

_____1. The smallest unit in the body is a cell.

_____2. Some cells are nerve cells.

_____3. There is only one kind of cell in the human body.

_____4. Each kind of cell has a different job.

_____5. All cells are the same basic shape.

_____6. Every second, millions of old cells die and new cells replace them.

_____7. The average cell is about 1/100 of an inch across.

_____8. Cells are different sizes.

Amazing Systems

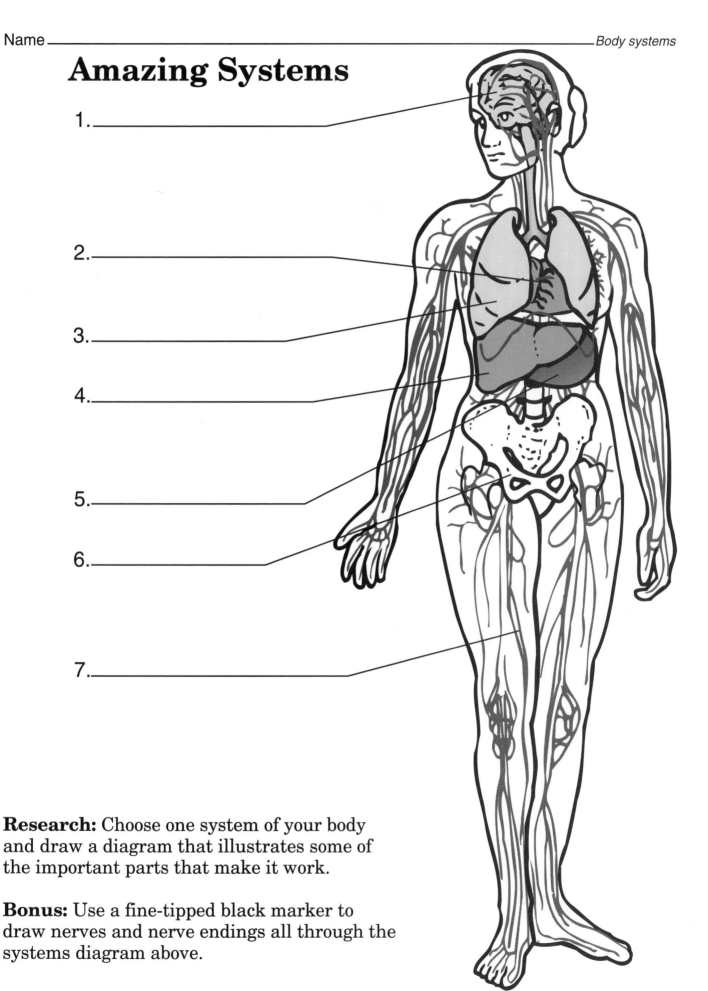

1. _____

2. _____

3. _____

4. _____

5. _____

6. _____

7. _____

Research: Choose one system of your body and draw a diagram that illustrates some of the important parts that make it work.

Bonus: Use a fine-tipped black marker to draw nerves and nerve endings all through the systems diagram above.

Amazing Systems

Billions of cells in your body work smoothly together.

Your body is an amazing group of systems. Each system has a specific function like a player on a baseball team with a specific task. For example, a pitcher's job is to throw the ball to the catcher who catches it.

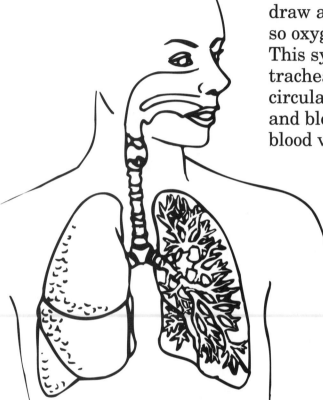

Similarly, the job of the respiratory system is to draw air into the body and remove carbon dioxide so oxygen can be carried throughout the body. This system includes the nasal cavity, pharynx, trachea, bronchi, lungs, and diaphragm. Then the circulatory system does the job of carrying oxygen and blood around your body. It includes the heart, blood vessels, lymph vessels, and lymph glands.

Your skeletal system and your muscular system help you move. These systems include all of your bones and muscles and everything that connects them. In your body are many systems that cooperate with each other to make you a fine-tuned working body!

Directions: Use the number code to label and color the diagram of body systems on page 10.

1. Use a blue crayon to color the **brain** (part of the nervous and sensory systems).
2. Use an orange crayon to color the **heart** (part of the circulatory system).
3. Use a green crayon to color the **lungs** (part of the respiratory system).
4. Use a yellow crayon to color the **liver** (part of the digestive system).
5. Use a purple crayon to color the **stomach** (part of the digestive system).
6. Use a pink crayon to color the **pelvis** (part of the skeletal system).
7. Use a red crayon to color the **veins** and **arteries** (part of the circulatory system).

Looking Through The Microscope

Directions: Unscramble the words to complete the sentences.

1. Van Leeuwenhoek studied (d o l b o) (l s l e c)_____
   under the microscope.

2. The (p m c o r i e c o s)_____ enables scientists to look at
   living things and study them in minute detail.

3. The microscope enables us to see (t b r i a c e a)_____.

4. The microscope has helped us make tremendous advances in
   (i e c c s n e)_____.

5. The microscope makes it possible for us to study the (e s c a s u)_____
   of diseases.

Research: Look at three different substances under a microscope or magnifying glass. Compare the way they look magnified. Write a few sentences about this.

Bonus: Look at a leaf under a microscope. If a microscope isn't available, use a magnifying glass. How is looking at a leaf under a microscope or magnifying glass different from looking at the leaf with your naked eye? Write a few sentences about what you saw through the microscope or magnifying glass that you couldn't see with your naked eye. What are the advantages of being able to study a small object enlarged?

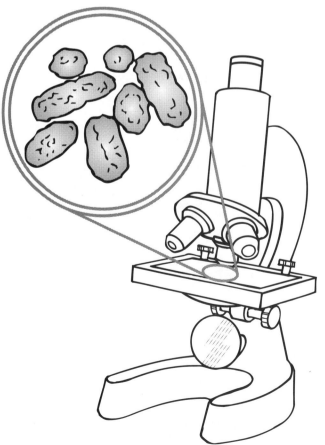

Looking Through The Microscope

Have you ever looked through a microscope? Electron microscopes can magnify cells up to 500,000 times!

In the middle of the 17th century, a merchant named van Leeuwenhoek used a small, beadlike lens to magnify objects up to 200 times. He used his discovery to study blood cells. With more and more powerful lenses, the microscope has made it possible to see living things in minute detail.

Today electron microscopes can magnify cells up to 500,000 times! Modern microscopes allow scientists to see bacteria and study the causes of diseases. The microscope has helped us learn much more about the human body. It has opened the door to many advances in medicine and science.

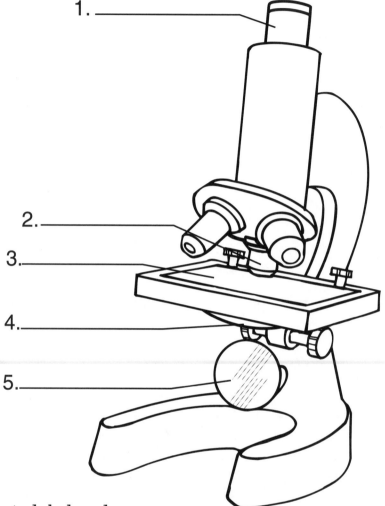

Directions: Use the number code to label and color each part of the microscope.

1. Color the **eyepiece** yellow.

2. Color the **lens** orange.

3. Color the **glass slide** red. (The object being studied rests on it.)

4. Color the **condenser lens** purple. (It focuses a beam of light onto the object being studied.)

5. Color the **mirror** red. (A strong beam of light strikes the mirror and shines from below onto the object being studied.)

Understanding The Human Body

Directions: Circle the letter of the best answer for each question.

1. What does *dissect* mean?
   - (a) examine carefully
   - (b) carefully cut apart
   - (c) both a and b

2. Before the 15th and 16th centuries, study of the body was done mostly by
   - (a) dissection
   - (b) using X rays
   - (c) observation

3. Which word in the text means "so great it is hard to believe"?
   - (a) incredible
   - (b) vital
   - (c) observation

4. When did dissection become an important technique for studying the body?
   - (a) before the European Renaissance
   - (b) after the European Renaissance
   - (c) around 1800

5. In the text, the word *organ* means
   - (a) a musical instrument
   - (b) a part of the body
   - (c) a means by which things are done

Research: Find out about X rays. When were they first used? Who discovered the process?

Bonus: Use your observation skills. Get an apple or an orange. Write two sentences that describe how the piece of fruit looks. Then use a plastic, serrated knife to cut the fruit in half. Look at it again. Note how much more of the fruit you can see when you go beneath the "skin." Write two sentences that tell about something you can see after dissecting the fruit that you couldn't see before. Cut the fruit halves in half again. Examine these pieces. Compare what you saw after the first and second cuts.

Understanding The Human Body

How do we know that your body is 70–85% water?

Did you know that the study of the structure of the body is called *anatomy?* Knowledge of how the body functions is called *physiology*. Physiologists study all the body's organs, glands, chemicals, and vital functions.

In early history, the body was studied mostly by observation. After the 15th and 16th centuries—a time known as the European Renaissance—the body was cut open, dissected, and then studied. What incredible advances have been made since then!

Today physicians and scientists can use X rays to look inside the human body. They can study human cells with microscopes and computer-generated models.

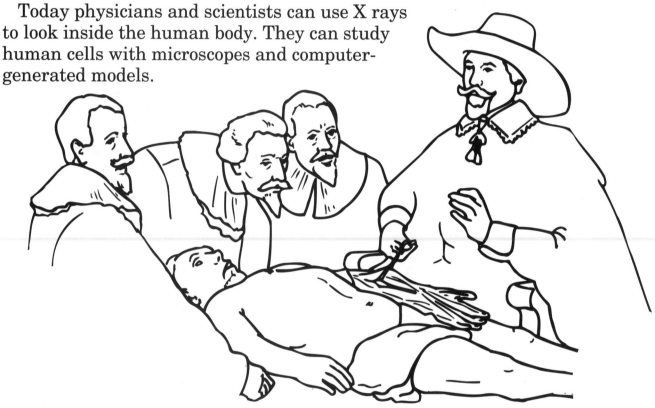

Directions: Circle the letter of the best answer for each question.

1. What is the study of a body's structure called?
   (a) anatomy   (b) physiology   (c) chemistry

2. What is the study of the body's organs, glands, chemicals, and vital functions called?
   (a) anatomy   (b) physiology   (c) chemistry

3. Scientists studying human tissues discovered that your body is 70–85%
   (a) water   (b) organs and glands   (c) blood

Building Blocks

Did you know you have billions of cells in your body? Every second, millions of cells in your body die and are replaced with new ones!

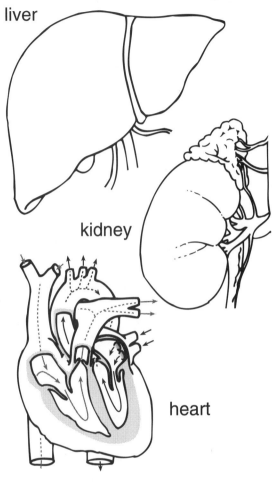

liver

kidney

heart

Cells are the building blocks and the workhorses of your body. You have about 200 different kinds of cells. Although the average human cell is only about 1/1,000 inch wide, these tiny cells have tremendous jobs to do! Some cells fight disease, some transport oxygen, and some produce movement. Some cells make proteins, chemicals, or liquids. Some cells store nutrients. Others are responsible for your thoughts, emotions, and memories. Some cells can even combine to create another human being.

You have billions of cells in your body. Similar cells form *tissue*. Tissues, in turn, form *organs*, which are the major body parts. The heart, liver, kidneys, and lungs are examples of organs. The organs work together as a system. Each system has a specific job in your body.

Directions: Circle the letter of the best answer for each question.

1. Cells are the building blocks and workhorses for
   (a) tall buildings   (b) the body   (c) farms

2. Approximately how many different kinds of cells are in the body?
   (a) 2   (b) 20   (c) 200

3. Every second, millions of cells in your body
   (a) die   (b) are replaced by new ones   (c) both a and b

4. How big is the average cell?
   (a) 100 cells equal an inch.   (b) 1,000 cells equal an inch.
   (c) 10 cells equal an inch.

Building Blocks

Directions: Write a complete sentence to answer each question.

1. What forms body tissue?_____

_____

2. Give some examples of organs._____

_____

3. How do organs work together?_____

_____

4. Describe cells._____

_____

5. Name three functions for cells of the body. _____

_____

_____

_____

6. How many different kinds of cells are in the body?_____

_____

Research: Draw a simple cell. Include the following: *nucleolus, nucleus, cell membrane, nuclear membrane,* and *cytoplasm.* Label and color each part.

Bonus: Make a graph to show the life span of the following kinds of cells:
intestine lining—6 days
taste buds—7 days
red blood cells—120 days
bone cells—3,600 to 11,000 days
nerve cells—7,000 to 50,000 days

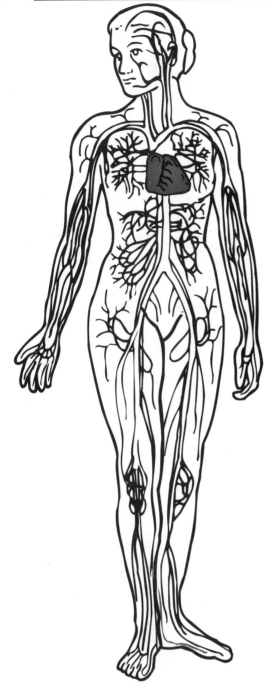

An Efficient System

When you reach adulthood, your heart will beat more than 100,000 times each day!

The *circulatory system* has two important jobs. It moves blood and regulates the temperature of your body. The circulatory system—which is made up of your heart, blood vessels, and blood—carries nutrients, oxygen, antibodies, and hormones to the cells of your body. The heart is the pump that keeps your blood moving through the blood vessels. On its journey, blood picks up oxygen from the lungs and nutrients from the digestive system.

Because you are a warm-blooded animal, your body has a fairly steady body temperature. Your circulatory system helps maintain this constant temperature. Warmer blood from the center of your body is brought to the surface to be cooled. The circulatory system does all of this work with about four to five quarts of blood.

Directions: Use words or short phrases to answer the questions.

1. Name the system that carries blood throughout the body._____

2. List three things that make up the circulatory system._____

_____

3. Name two functions of the circulatory system._____

_____

An Efficient System

Directions: Use words or short phrases to answer the questions.

1. Name the body parts that carry blood._____

_____

2. The blood picks up oxygen from which body parts?_____

_____

3. What does the blood pick up from the digestive system?_____

_____

4. Where does the blood take oxygen and nutrients?_____

_____

5. How is warmer blood from the center of your body cooled?_____

_____

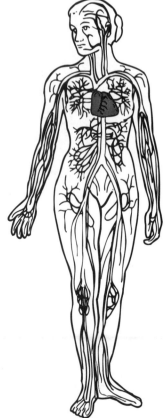

Research: Who is Barney Clark? What courageous thing did he do that advanced medical study of the heart?

Bonus: To find out how many times per minute your heart beats, take your pulse. (Place two fingertips of your right hand on the underside of your left wrist just below the base of your thumb.) Sit quietly for one minute and count the pulse beats. Using this number, figure out approximately how many times your heart will beat in one hour and in 24 hours.

Tubes For Carrying Blood

If your blood vessels were laid end to end, they would stretch around the equator 2 1/2 times!

Blood is pushed through the circulatory system by the pumping action of your heart. It travels in tubes called *blood vessels*.

There are only three kinds of blood vessels: *arteries, veins,* and *capillaries*. The arteries carry blood, rich with oxygen and nutrients, away from the heart. Veins carry blood back to the heart for fresh oxygen from the lungs. Veins are thinner than arteries. Capillaries are even smaller. Capillaries are tiny blood vessels that carry blood between the smallest arteries and the smallest veins.

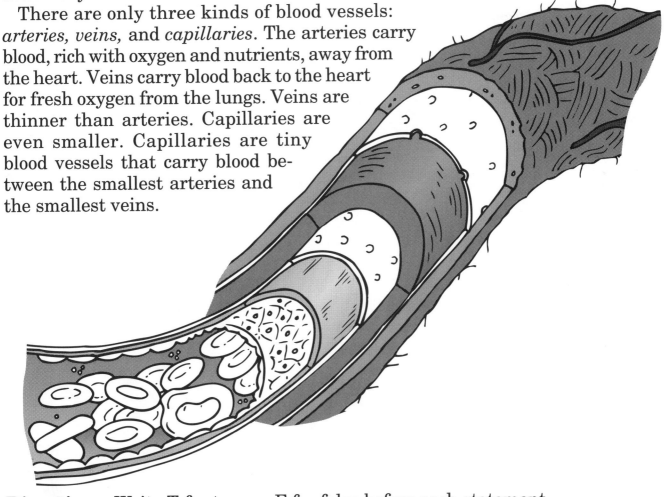

Directions: Write T for true or F for false before each statement.

_____1. Blood is propelled through the body by the pumping action of the heart.

_____2. There are three kinds of blood vessels: arteries, veins, and capillaries.

_____3. Arteries carry blood that is rich with carbon dioxide away from the heart.

_____4. Capillaries are the largest blood vessels.

_____5. Veins are wider than arteries.

Tubes For Carrying Blood

Directions: Label the arrows and color the diagram of blood moving to and from the heart.

1. **Arteries** carry blood away from the heart. Color the arteries red.
2. **Veins** carry blood to the heart. Color the veins blue.
3. Color the **capillaries** yellow.

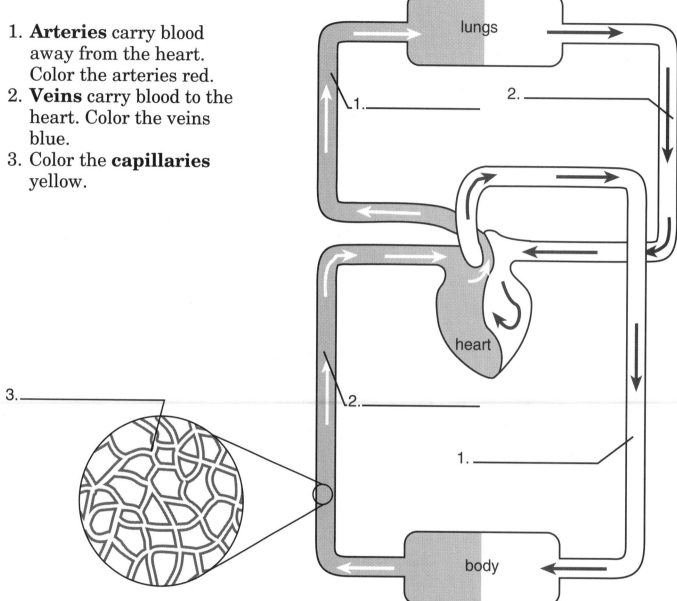

Research: Find out how the diameters of arteries, veins, and capillaries compare in size. Draw a picture of a cross-section of each that shows its size in relationship to the others.

Bonus: On another sheet of paper, draw the outline of a body. Then add a picture of the heart. Next draw tubes to represent arteries going from the heart to the arms and legs and brain. Color them red. Draw tubes to represent veins going back to the heart and color them blue. Draw yellow lines to represent capillaries. Check the text to see which lines should be drawn the largest and the smallest.

Oxygen And Nutrient Carrier

Your blood cells rush around the body faster than race cars at the Indianapolis 500! The heart pumps blood so fast that it takes only a minute for each blood cell to travel all the way around your body.

Blood consists of *red cells*, *white cells*, *platelets*, and *plasma*. Each part of your blood has a specialized job. Your *red blood cells* are disc-shaped and carry oxygen to all parts of your body. The *white blood cells* fight disease. Some white blood cells are able to destroy bacteria and other foreign particles in your body. Tiny fragments called *platelets* are important in blood clotting. Platelets rupture and release enzymes that promote blood clotting.

Blood is made up of about 55% plasma, 43% red blood cells, and 2% white blood cells. *Plasma* is the fluid part of blood. It is yellowish and about 90% water. You have about nine pints of blood in your body.

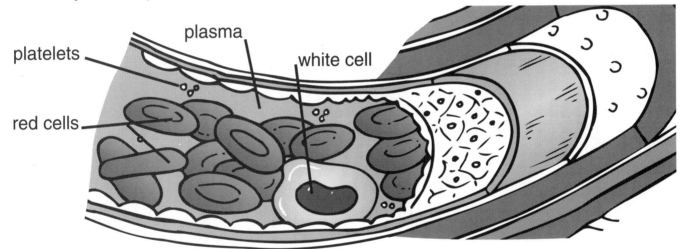

Directions: Use a number from the text to answer each question, or research to find the answer for each question.

1. What percentage of your blood is plasma? _____

2. What percentage of your blood is white blood cells? _____

3. What percentage of blood plasma is water? _____

4. What percentage of your blood works to carry oxygen throughout your body? _____

_____

5. What percentage of plasma is not water? _____

Oxygen And Nutrient Carrier

In a laboratory test tube, blood can be separated into its parts. The heaviest part of the blood, which is also the largest amount, is at the bottom. The next heaviest part is above that, and the lightest part is on the top.

Directions: Can you tell from the text which part is the red blood cells? Color the red blood cells red. Leave the part that shows the white blood cells white, and color the plasma yellow. Label each part.

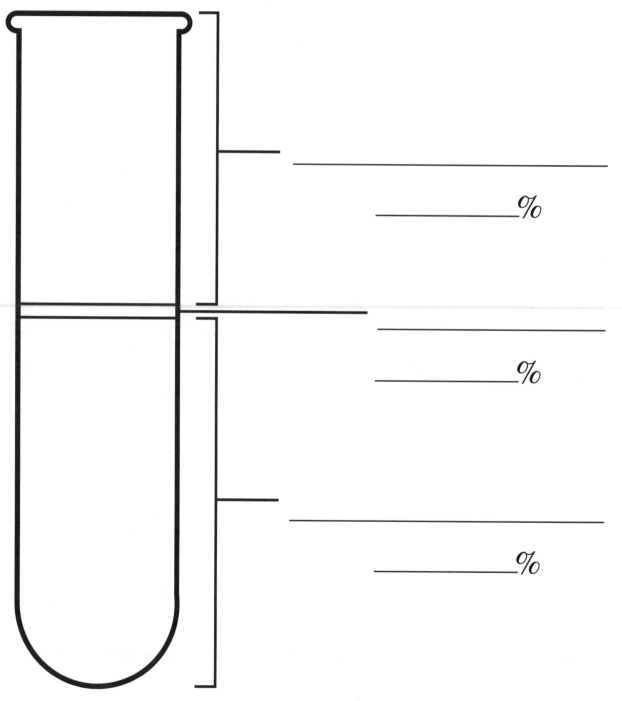

_____

_____%

_____

_____%

_____

_____%

A Busy Pump

There are approximately nine pints of blood circulating through your body.

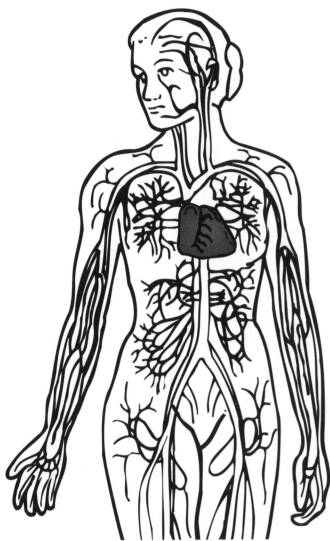

If your heart stopped beating, you would die. Why? Because your heart pumps blood full of oxygen and food to your body's cells. You cannot live without oxygen and food.

Your heart is a hollow muscle. It's about the size of your fist. It weighs about nine ounces. The heart consists of four chambers—two thin-walled *atria* (*auricles*) and two powerful, muscled *ventricles*.

The heart works like two pumps with alternating rhythms. The right side of the heart consists of the right atrium and ventricle. The right side receives blood from the great veins known as the *inferior* and *superior venae cavae* and pumps blood to the lungs. As the blood passes through the lungs, it takes on oxygen and gives up carbon dioxide. The left side of the heart receives blood full of oxygen from the lungs and pumps it through the *aorta* into the arteries.

Directions: Use words from the text to complete the statements.

1. Your heart is a _____ muscle.

2. Your heart is about the size of your _____ .

3. Your heart weighs about _____ .

4. You have about _____ pints of blood circulating in your body.

5. Your heart pumps blood full of oxygen and _____ to the body's cells.

A Busy Pump

Directions: Use the number code to label and color the diagram of the heart.

■ ■ ■ ■ Deoxygenated blood
(blood lacking oxygen)

▬ ▬ ▬ ▬ Oxygenated blood
(blood carrying oxygen)

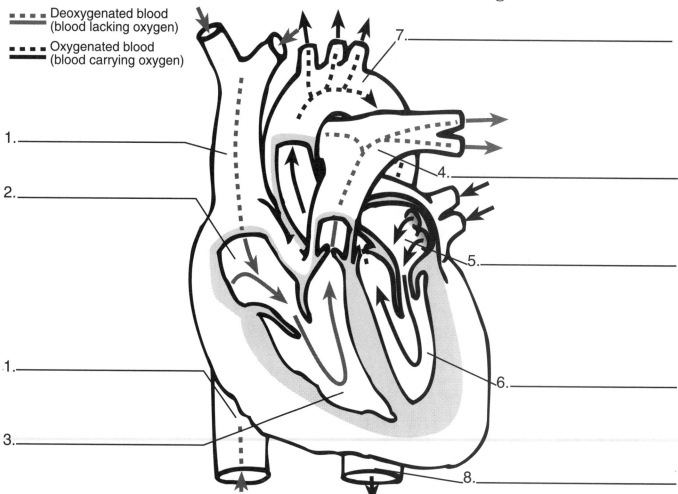

7._____

1._____

2._____

4._____

5._____

1._____

6._____

3._____

8._____

1. The **superior (upper) vena cava** and the **inferior (lower) vena cava** carry used blood into the right side of the heart. Color them red.
2. The **right atrium** receives blood from the inferior and superior venae cavae. Color it orange.
3. The **right ventricle** is a powerful, muscled part of your heart that receives blood from the right atrium, then pumps it through the pulmonary artery. Color it yellow.
4. The **pulmonary artery** splits into two branches that carry blood from the right ventricle of the heart to the lungs. Color the pulmonary artery blue.
5. The **left atrium** receives blood from the lungs and pumps it into the left ventricle. Color the left atrium orange.
6. The **left ventricle** then pumps the blood through the aorta. Color the left ventricle yellow.
7. The **aortic arch** is a curved blood vessel that becomes the **dorsal aorta**. From it arteries branch to the head and neck. Color the aortic arch purple.
8. Blood travels to the bottom half of the body through the **descending aorta**. Color it purple.

Tiny Tubes

**There are ten billion (10,000,000,000) capillaries in your body.
That is nearly three times the population of the whole world!**

    Your heart rate can be measured by feeling the pulse in the artery of your wrist. Can you feel your artery pulse? Now, look at your arm and find a vein. Veins and arteries are like main highways. They carry blood to and from the heart, respectively. The capillaries—tiny connections found between arteries and veins—are where the blood does its work of exchanging fresh blood for old. Your capillaries are too small to see.

    When you get a black-and-blue bruise, capillaries under the skin have been injured and broken. The color of blood changes from red to purple to blue to green and, finally, to yellow.

Directions: Place two fingertips of your right hand on the underside of your left wrist just below the base of your thumb. Then watch a clock for 60 seconds and count the number of pulsations. That is your beginning heart rate. Complete each activity. After each one, time your heart rate in the same manner and record it on the graph.

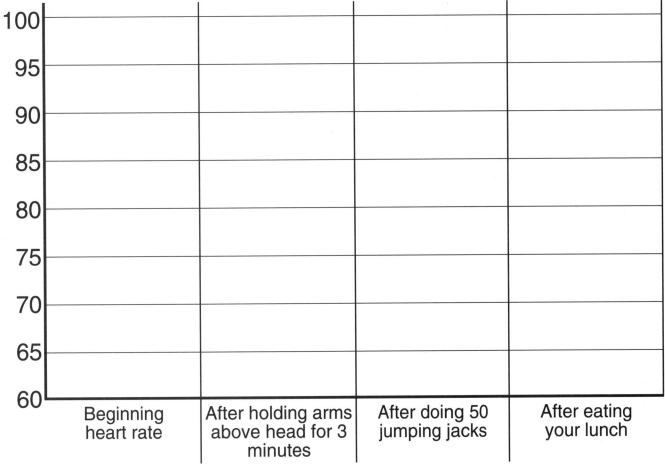

Beginning heart rate	After holding arms above head for 3 minutes	After doing 50 jumping jacks	After eating your lunch

Tiny Tubes

Directions: Write T for true or F for false before each statement.

_____1. If you look carefully at your arm, you may see a vein.

_____2. You can feel your artery pulse.

_____3. If you look hard, you can see tiny capillaries through your skin.

_____4. There are very few capillaries in your body.

_____5. Arteries and veins are bigger than capillaries.

_____6. Arteries carry blood from the heart.

_____7. In the text, the word *highways* means "surfaces covered with blacktop."

_____8. Capillaries are bigger than veins and arteries.

_____9. Capillaries connect arteries and veins.

_____10. Capillaries are where fresh blood is exchanged for old.

Research: Look up *blood clot.* Why is it necessary for your blood to clot? What happens if your blood doesn't clot? Write a short paragraph about this process.

Germ Busters

Bacteria are one-celled organisms that can be seen only when magnified thousands of times under a microscope.

Do you know that blood is not the only fluid that circulates in your body? You also have *lymph*. This is a milky liquid that travels around the body in its own set of tubes. Lymph is important because it carries white blood cells around the body to fight infection.

Lymph also collects waste from the cells. Like blood, lymph distributes nutrients. The lymph vessels have little pockets, which are glands. These are called *lymph nodes*. The nodes are where dead germs collect during an illness. Do you remember having a sore throat and feeling lumps on both sides of your throat? Those lumps were your enlarged lymph nodes.

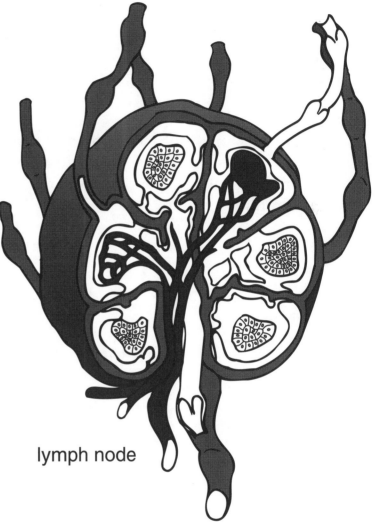

lymph node

Directions: Use words from the text to complete the sentences.

1. Lymph collects _____ from the cells.

2. Dead germs collect in the _____ nodes.

3. White blood cells fight _____ .

4. Lymph vessels have little pockets, which are _____ .

5. Lymph carries _____ blood cells around the body.

Germ Busters

Directions: Use the clues and the text to fill in the crossword puzzle.

Across:
1. what a lymph node is
3. what lymph collects from cells
5. a milky liquid that carries white cells that fight germs
6. another name for *liquid*

Down:
1. what collects in lymph nodes during illness
2. what circulates in the body carrying oxygen and food
3. color of blood cells that fight infection
4. what lymph travels in

Research: What are *antibodies?* In a few sentences, describe antibodies.

Bonus: Make a list of diseases. How many can you write? Can you list ten? Twenty? Fifty? Put a star by each of the diseases you have had.

Shaped Like A Bean

About 2 1/2 pints of blood are pumped through the kidneys every minute. That is more than a quart!

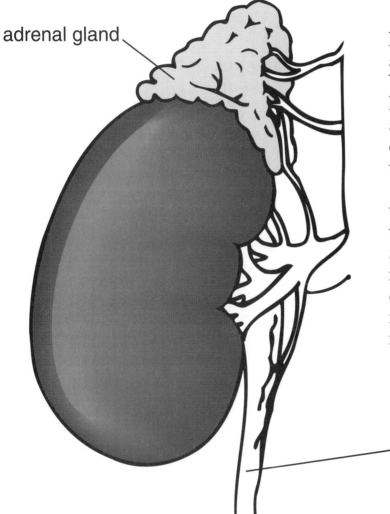

adrenal gland

ureters (connects to bladder)

Do you know why kidney beans have that name? It's because they are shaped like your body's *kidneys*. You have two kidneys. They are located on each side of your spine, above your waist, behind your abdominal cavity. Two tubes connect the kidneys with the *bladder*.

The kidneys filter waste from the blood. This waste combines with water to form a fluid called *urine*. The tiny units in the kidneys that filter the blood are called *nephrons*. Each kidney has more than one million (1,000,000) nephrons.

Directions: Unscramble the words to complete the sentences.

1. Most people have two (s y d k i n e)_____.

2. Tubes (c c n t o e n)_____ the kidneys with the bladder.

3. The kidneys (i l f r e t)_____waste from the blood.

4. (n i u r e)_____is made in the kidneys.

5. Nephrons are the (t s i n u)_____ that filter waste from the blood in the kidneys.

Shaped Like A Bean

Directions: Use the clues and the text to fill in the crossword puzzle.

Across:
1. Kidneys are above your waist and behind your
   _____ cavity.
3. Your kidneys filter_____ from your blood.
5. The tiny units in the kidneys that filter the blood are
   called_____ .
7. Kidney beans are shaped like your body's_____ .

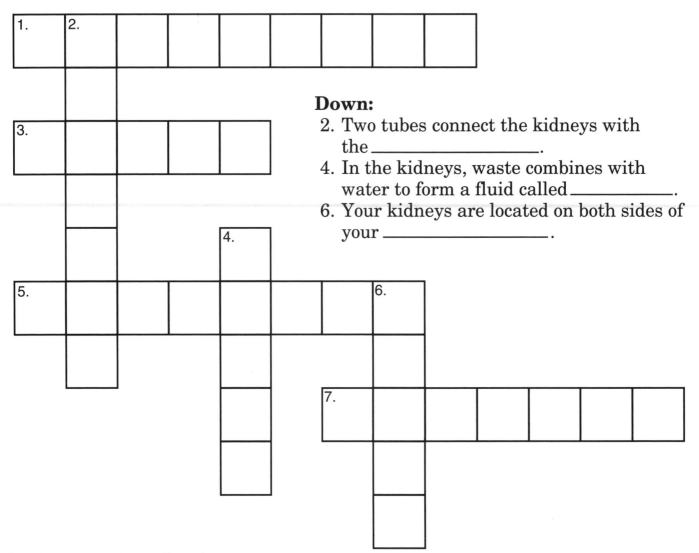

Down:
2. Two tubes connect the kidneys with
   the_____ .
4. In the kidneys, waste combines with
   water to form a fluid called_____ .
6. Your kidneys are located on both sides of
   your _____ .

Research: What is *dialysis?* Describe it in a few sentences.

Bonus: Have you ever eaten kidney pie? Make a list of internal organs of animals that some people eat.

A Breathtaking System

An adult's lungs can hold five quarts of air! How large a balloon do you think it would take to hold that much air?

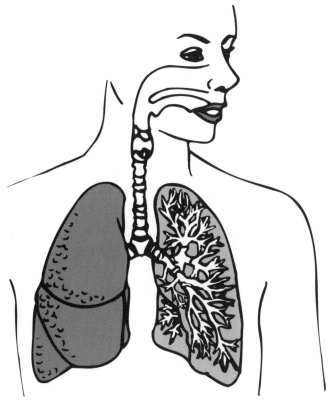

When you breathe in air through your nose and mouth, you get oxygen. You need oxygen to live. The air goes down your *windpipe* and into your lungs. Your lungs absorb oxygen from the air. The oxygen travels in the blood to every part of the body.

Your body uses oxygen to burn food and to give you energy. You make carbon dioxide when you do this. The blood carries the carbon dioxide back to the lungs. Then it is breathed out. This whole process is called *respiration.*

Directions: Use one word from the text to complete the statements.

1. You need_____ to live.

2. You take in air through the nose or the_____.

3. The air you breathe in goes down your_____and into your lungs.

4. The words in the text that mean "to inhale" are_____.

5. The oxygen you breathe in travels in the _____ to every part of your body.

6. When you breathe in, you take in _____.

7. When you breathe out, you get rid of _____.

8. Your body uses oxygen to burn _____.

9. The blood carries the carbon dioxide back to the lungs, and it is _____ out.

10. The process of breathing in and out is called _____.

A Breathtaking System

Directions: Use the number code to label and color the diagram of the respiratory system.

1. You take in air through your **nasal passage.** Color it green.
2. The **pharynx** connects your mouth and nasal passages. Color it yellow.
3. The **epiglottis** is the flap of cartilage behind your tongue. It helps close the opening to your windpipe when you swallow. Color it red.
4. The **larynx** is made of muscle and cartilage. It is where your **vocal cords** are located. Color it brown.
5. The **trachea** is a tube that serves as the main passageway for air to and from the lungs. Color it purple.
6. The **alveoli** are tiny air sacs at the ends of the **bronchioles.** Color them red.
7. The **diaphragm** is a wall of muscle and connecting tissue. Color it gray.
8. The **lungs** absorb oxygen from the air you breathe. Color the left lung blue.

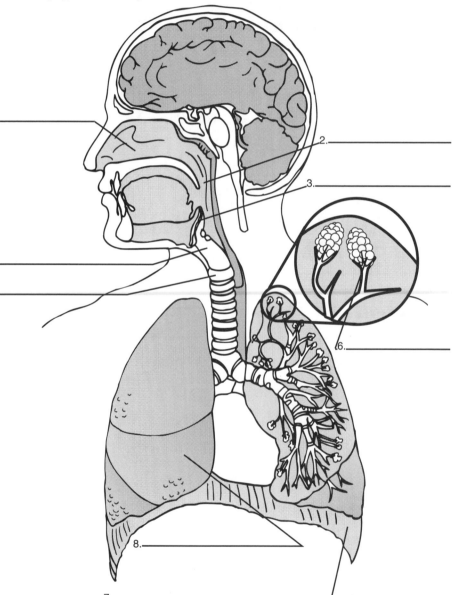

Research: Your right and left lungs are not identical. Find out how they are different.

Bonus: Sit quietly and listen to your breathing. Count how many times you breathe in and out each minute. Stand up and do 25 jumping jacks. Then count your breaths again. How does exercise affect breathing? Write a true statement about this.

The Nose Knows

Did you know you cannot sneeze with your eyes open?

The walls of your nose are lined with fine hairs. These hairs filter out dust and dirt. Your *nostrils* lead to two *nasal cavities* separated by a thin *nasal septum* made of cartilage and bone. The *nasal lining* warms the air you breathe and makes it moist. Your nose also protects a small patch of cells on the roof of the nasal cavity. These cells can detect about 4,000 different odors. The message for each odor is sent to the brain by a special nerve called the *olfactory nerve*. The brain interprets the odor and tells you how to react to it.

People prefer certain odors. It is said that the sense of smell is the sense that brings back forgotten memories more distinctly than any other sense. Do you remember pleasant memories when you smell certain things?

Directions: Ask ten people to rate each of the following odors with 10 being extremely pleasant and 1 being unpleasant. Write their ratings and yours on the chart. Answer the questions.

	Chocolate	Popcorn	Coffee	Orange peel	Roses	Gasoline	Dill pickles	Pipe tobacco	Onion	Smoke
#1										
#2										
#3										
#4										
#5										
#6										
#7										
#8										
#9										
#10										
You										

1. What was the most pleasant odor?_____

2. What was the most unpleasant odor?_____

The Nose Knows

Directions: Use the clues and the text to fill in the crossword puzzle.

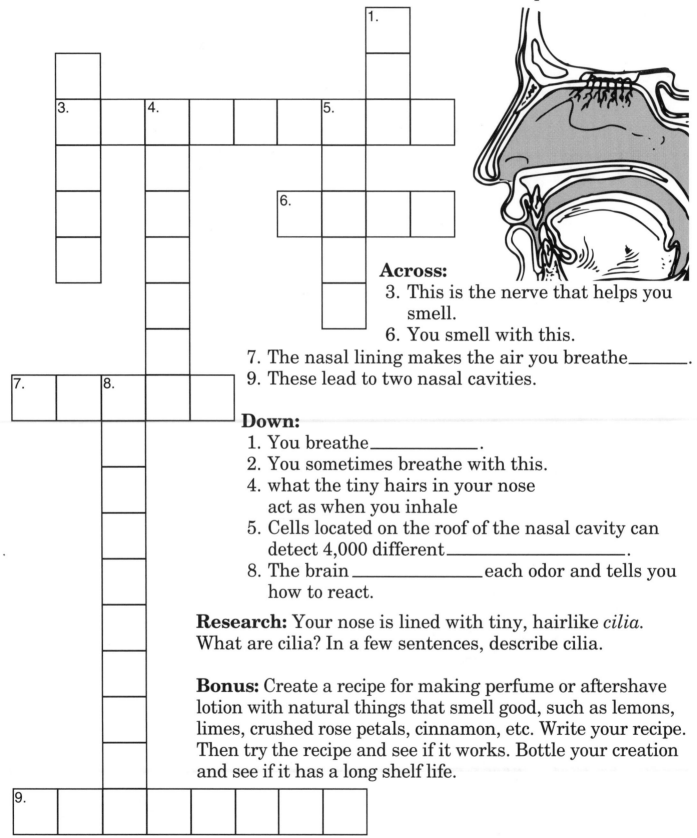

Across:

3. This is the nerve that helps you smell.
6. You smell with this.
7. The nasal lining makes the air you breathe_____.
9. These lead to two nasal cavities.

Down:

1. You breathe_____.
2. You sometimes breathe with this.
4. what the tiny hairs in your nose act as when you inhale
5. Cells located on the roof of the nasal cavity can detect 4,000 different_____.
8. The brain_____each odor and tells you how to react.

Research: Your nose is lined with tiny, hairlike *cilia*. What are cilia? In a few sentences, describe cilia.

Bonus: Create a recipe for making perfume or aftershave lotion with natural things that smell good, such as lemons, limes, crushed rose petals, cinnamon, etc. Write your recipe. Then try the recipe and see if it works. Bottle your creation and see if it has a long shelf life.

Catch Your Breath!

Your breathing rate increases automatically if you exercise vigorously.

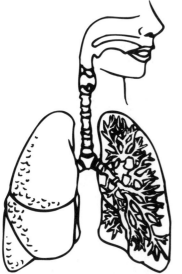

Air enters your lungs through your *windpipe.* The air then passes through the *bronchial tree* to the *alveoli.* In the alveoli there is an exchange of gases between the air and the blood.

Your breathing is automatic. You don't have to do anything or even be aware of it. Breathing centers in the base of your brain receive nerve impulses from your lungs. As the carbon dioxide in the blood increases, the brain sends a message to the breathing centers to increase your breathing rate.

Directions: Find a partner. Sitting quietly, breathe normally. Count how many times your partner breathes each minute for ten minutes. Have your partner count your breaths, too. Fill in the blanks.

Number of breaths after 1 minute _____

Number of breaths after 2 minutes _____

Number of breaths after 3 minutes _____

Number of breaths after 4 minutes _____

Number of breaths after 5 minutes _____

Number of breaths after 6 minutes _____

Number of breaths after 7 minutes _____

Number of breaths after 8 minutes _____

Number of breaths after 9 minutes _____

Number of breaths after 10 minutes _____

Name _____

Catch Your Breath!

Directions: Use the number code to label and color the diagram of the breathing mechanism.

1. Color the **alveoli** purple.
2. Color the **alveolus** surrounded by capillaries red.
3. Color the right **lung** yellow.
4. Color the left **lung** orange.
5. Color the **trachea** green.
6. Color the **diaphragm** blue.

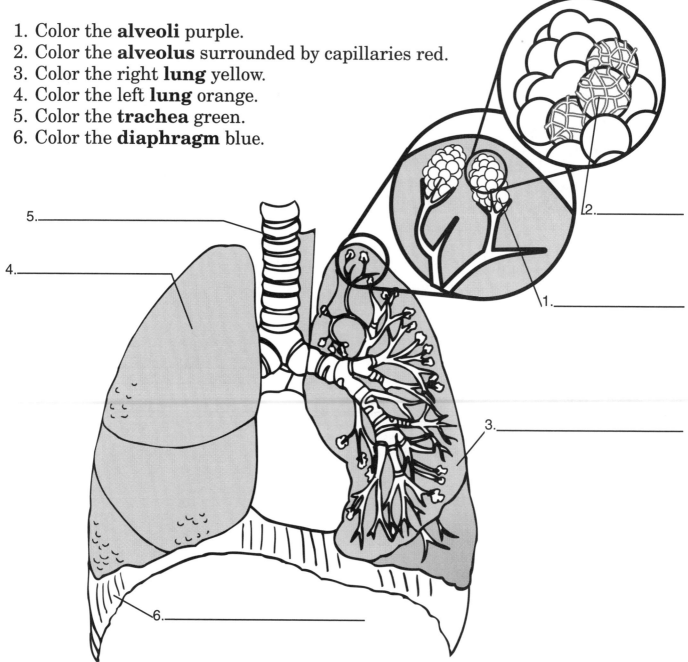

Research: Find out about the *Hering-Breur reflex*. Write a sentence about it.

Bonus: Ask a parent or sibling to count and record how many breaths you take each minute for ten minutes while you are sleeping. How does this compare to the number you took while you were awake? Jump rope for three minutes. Then count and record the number of breaths you take each minute for ten minutes. How does the number of breaths per minute change over the ten-minute period?

Saved By A Skeleton!

You were born with 350 bones. By the time you are an adult, you will have only about 206 bones.

Do you know what protects all the systems of your body? Bones! Your heart is protected by ribs that form a cage around your heart and lungs. Your skull protects your brain from injury, and your backbone protects your spinal cord.

When you were born, you had 350 soft bones. Many were more like *cartilage* than hard bone. As children grow, the bones that are mostly this translucent, elastic tissue will be replaced by hard, bony tissue. This process is called *ossification*. By the time you are an adult, you will have only 206 different bones. These bones will be hard and made of calcium and phosphorus. All of your bones together are called your *skeleton*.

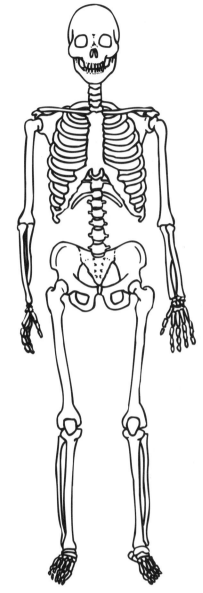

Directions: Use words or numbers from the text to complete the statements.

1. The bones that protect the heart are the _____.

2. The ribs form a_____around the heart and lungs.

3. The backbone protects the _____.

4. The_____protects the brain.

5. When you were born, you had _____ soft bones.

6. The hard parts of bones are made of calcium and_____ .

7. All your bones together are called a_____.

8. Most adults have_____bones in their bodies.

Saved By A Skeleton!

Directions: Hidden in the word-search puzzle are 15 words from the text. The words are written vertically and horizontally. How many of the 15 can you find? There are other words in the puzzle that are not in the text, but they don't count. Find and circle only words from the text.

```
p   h   o   s   p   h   o   r   u   s   s

h   e   a   r   t   b   o   n   c   c   k

c   s   b   i   e   i   s   b   a   o   e

o   k   o   b   o   n   e   s   l   l   l

r   u   d   s   l   j   b   p   c   l   e

d   l   y   l   u   u   r   i   i   a   t

l   l   e   u   n   r   a   n   u   p   o

u   n   s   n   g   y   i   a   m   s   n

c   a   g   e   s   s   n   l   l   e   g

p   r   o   t   e   c   t   s   u   n   s
```

Research: What happens when you break a bone? Talk to a doctor or read an encyclopedia to find out how bones mend.

Bonus: Choose ten words from the text and create a word-search puzzle using those words.

Big Bones And Little Bones

The stirrup bone, the smallest bone in your body, is located inside your ear. It is only 7/100 inch long!

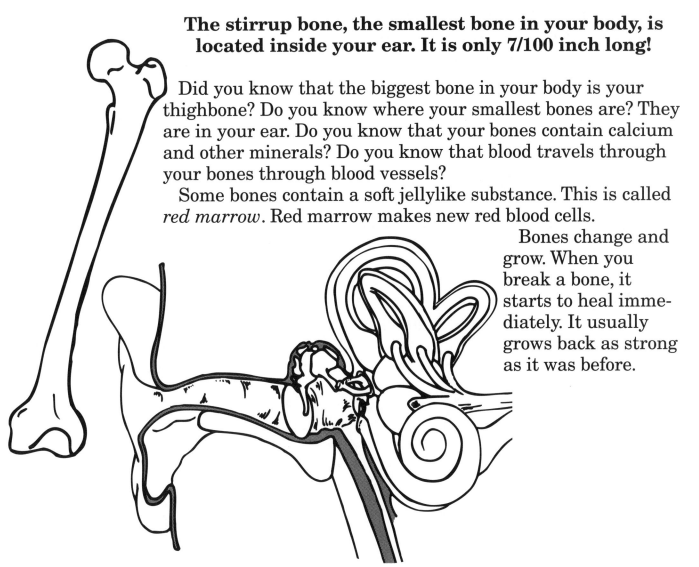

Did you know that the biggest bone in your body is your thighbone? Do you know where your smallest bones are? They are in your ear. Do you know that your bones contain calcium and other minerals? Do you know that blood travels through your bones through blood vessels?

Some bones contain a soft jellylike substance. This is called *red marrow*. Red marrow makes new red blood cells.

Bones change and grow. When you break a bone, it starts to heal immediately. It usually grows back as strong as it was before.

Directions: Write a complete sentence to answer each question.

1. What is the biggest bone in your body?

_____

2. Where is the smallest bone in your body?

_____

3. Explain how blood travels through your bones.

_____

Big Bones And Little Bones

Directions: Write a complete sentence to answer each question.

1. After a bone is broken, does it ever grow back as strong as it was before it was broken?

   _____

2. After you break a bone, how long is it before it begins to mend?

   _____

3. What do bones contain?

   _____

4. What is the soft substance in bones called?

   _____

5. What does red marrow do?

   _____

6. How does blood travel through your bones?

   _____

7. What is the most amazing fact you learned about bones?

   _____

Research: The thighbone accounts for about one-fourth of the height of an average person. Measure your height. Measure your thighbone from your hip to your knee. How do they compare? Measure the bones in your upper and lower arms and legs. Make a chart of these numbers.

Bonus: Sometimes when someone breaks a bone, the doctor forms a plaster cast around the bone to hold the bone in place. This is so it can heal without being disturbed. Other times, molded plastic casts or plastic-and-metal splints are used to support the bone while it is healing. Use a plastic or metal ruler and gauze strips to make a cast or splint on your wrist, finger, foot, ankle, or other bone. Be creative. Be prepared to tell the scientific name for the "broken" bone and how you broke it. Ouch!

Inside Bones

Your bones make over five billion (5,000,000,000) new red blood cells every day.

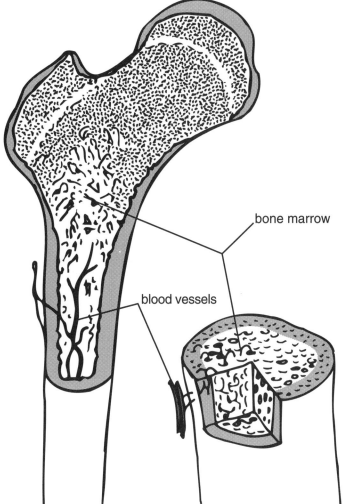

bone marrow

blood vessels

Bones are so hard that you may think of them as being solid like concrete. Wrong! The outer part of a bone is hard and dense. This outer part encloses a softer, spongy kind of material in some bones. Inside that—in some adult bones and in all baby bones—is *red marrow*.

Red marrow is a jellylike substance. Red marrow's job is to make red blood cells and some white blood cells. You have about half a pound of red marrow. Every second your bones make millions of red blood cells. Bones are also the storage places for minerals, especially calcium and phosphorus.

Directions: Unscramble the words to complete the sentences.

1. The outside of the bone is (d r h a)_____ and dense.

2. A spongy kind of material is (n i s d e i)_____ most bones.

3. Bones are storage places for (s a e i m n r l)_____.

4. Marrow is like (y l j e l)_____.

5. The job of red marrow is to make new (l b d o o)_____ cells.

Inside Bones

Directions: Hidden in the word-search puzzle are ten words from the text. The words are written vertically, horizontally, and diagonally. How many of the ten can you find? There are other words in the puzzle that are not in the text, but they don't count. Find and circle only words from the text.

s	o	l	i	d	g	z	b	m
p	u	r	c	h	q	b	o	a
o	d	b	a	b	y	p	n	r
n	x	e	s	o	f	t	e	r
g	n	m	n	t	w	y	t	o
y	g	i	x	s	a	k	p	w
y	l	e	y	d	e	n	f	k
a	d	u	l	t	s	y	c	u
j	c	o	n	c	r	e	t	e

Research: If possible, examine a large bone from a meat department that has been cut crosswise to show the layers of the bone. Wash, rinse, and dry the bone. Identify the *outer covering*, the *hard bone* (the tough and compact part), the *spongy bone* (the part that holds red marrow), and the *red marrow* (the soft inner center of the bone).

Bonus: Draw a cross-section of a bone that has a soft, spongy inside and red marrow inside that. Color each part a different color and label it. Compare your drawing with the drawings done by two friends.

Up And Down Your Spine

Because of gravity, your backbone compacts a little each day, making you a bit shorter at night than in the morning.

Your backbone, or *spine,* supports your body. The spine has 33 bones. These bones are stacked on top of each other with spongy cartilage disks between the bones. The bones are called *vertebrae.* You can bend, twist, and move because of your vertebrae. The top 24 vertebrae are in three sections—the neck, chest, and back.

The seven vertebrae in the neck are the smallest bones. They support your neck. They allow you to look at the ceiling, tuck your chin next to your chest, and turn your head from side to side.

The next 12 vertebrae form the chest section. Each of these vertebrae is attached to a pair of ribs. The next five vertebrae are the largest vertebrae. They make up the back section. These are followed by five more vertebrae *fused* together to form your *sacrum.* The last four vertebrae are also fused together. They form your *coccyx* or tailbone. Have you ever fallen and landed on your tailbone?

Many people have back pain because of injuries to their vertebrae. The spongy disks become less resilient with age. They may become damaged with improper or heavy lifting. A disk that is damaged can bulge out and press on nerves, causing pain. This is called a *slipped disk.*

Directions: Circle the letter of the best answer for each question.

1. The body is supported by
   (a) the neck   (b) the backbone   (c) the ribs

2. The backbone is a column of separate bones called vertebrae. How many are there?
   (a) 12   (b) 24   (c) 33

3. The vertebrae that form the backbone are
   (a) next to each other
   (b) not connected
   (c) on top of one another

Up And Down Your Spine

Directions: Use words or phrases to answer the questions.

1. The bones that make up the _____ are called *vertebrae*.

2. The smallest vertebrae are located in the _____ .

3. Name three things the vertebrae in your neck allow you to do.

_____

_____

_____

4. How many vertebrae are attached to the pairs of ribs? _____

5. Write the word in the text that means "closely and firmly packs together."

_____

6. Five vertebrae fused together form the _____ .

7. The last four vertebrae fused together are the _____ .

Research: What does it mean when a person has a *slipped disk?* Write a short paragraph about it.

Bonus: List five things that *send chills up and down your spine.* Name three *backbreaking* jobs. Name two things that are a *pain in the neck.*

The Tailbone

**Have you ever fallen on your tailbone? Do you know where it is?
It is at the very bottom of your backbone.**

The backbone is also called the *spinal column* or the *spine*. The spine supports your body, and it protects the *spinal cord*. There are two parts of the backbone that are solid bone. The first part is called the *sacrum*. It is connected to the *coccyx*, which most people call the *tailbone*. Your coccyx is at the base of your spine. It is made up of four small vertebrae that are fused together.

Directions: Use the number code to label and color the diagram of the spine.

1. The top 7 vertebrae of the spine are in the **neck.** They are the smallest vertebrae of the spine. Color them orange.
2. The next 12 vertebrae are the **chest** section. Color them red.
3. The last 5 vertebrae are the **back.** They are the largest vertebrae of the spine. Color them pink.
4. The **sacroiliac** is the joint that connects the sacrum with the upper vertebrae. Color it yellow.
5. The next 5 vertebrae are fused together. They form the **sacrum.** Color it purple.
6. The last 4 vertebrae are also fused and they form the **coccyx.** Color it green.

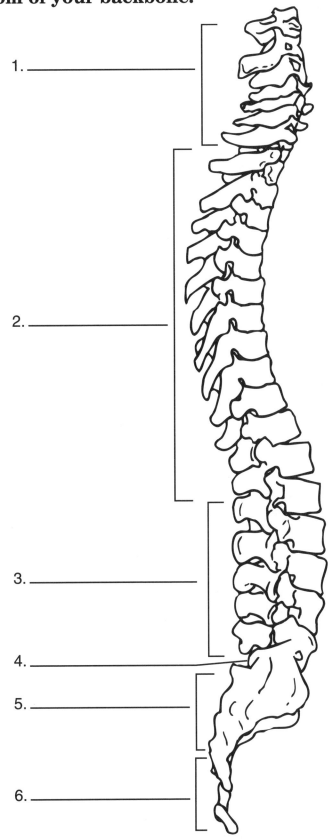

1. _____

2. _____

3. _____

4. _____

5. _____

6. _____

The Tailbone

Directions: Write a complete sentence to answer each question.

1. Where is your tailbone?

_____

2. Describe your spinal column.

_____

3. What is another name for the backbone?

_____

4. Name the joint that connects the sacrum with the upper vertebrae.

_____

5. What are the main functions of your spinal column?

Research: Feel the back of your neck and down the center of your back. Can you count the vertebrae that make up each section of your backbone? How can you prevent serious injury to your back? Illustrate the right way and the wrong way to lift a heavy object.

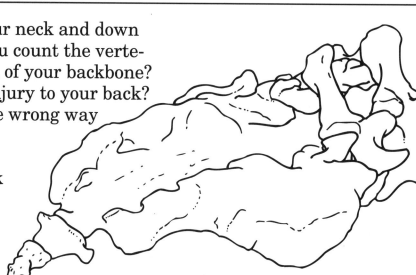

Bonus: Get 33 dominoes. Stack them on top of each other. Think about what you could do to move the dominoes as a stack without the stack falling apart. How would you connect them? What would happen if the dominoes at the bottom were smaller than the dominoes at the top? What would happen if the dominoes at the bottom were twice as big as the dominoes at the top? Write a few sentences about this experiment.

Fascinating Facts About The Human Body—Grades 4–6 • ©1995 The Education Center, Inc. • TEC370

Knee Knowledge

Do you know what parts of your skeleton work like hinges? These are your elbows and knees. The parts that make your knee and elbow joints—bones, muscles, ligaments, and tendons—allow you to run, walk, kick, and climb.

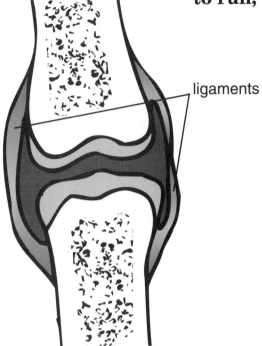

ligaments

The knee joins together the upper leg bone (thighbone) and the lower leg bone (tibia). It is one of the most mobile joints in your body.

The bones of the knee are held together by ligaments. Tendons fasten muscles to the bones. The force with which muscles contract pulls tendons with enormous power, but tendons do not tear. Tendons can withstand a tremendous amount of tension.

Directions: Use the clues and the word bank to help you label the bones on the diagram of the skeleton found on page 46.

Word Bank

cranium (top of the skull)

sternum (breastbone)

radius (lower arm bone)

metacarpal (hand bone)

patella (kneecap)

metatarsal (foot bone)

mandible (lower jaw)

humerus (bone of the upper arm)

carpal (wrist bone)

fibula (bone in the back of the lower leg)

scapula (shoulder blade)

rib (curved chest bone)

pelvis (hipbone)

femurs (thighbones)

tibia (front lower leg bone)

vertebra (one of the bones in the backbone)

clavicle (collarbone)

ulna (lower arm bone)

phalange (finger bone)

tarsal (anklebone)

Knee Knowledge

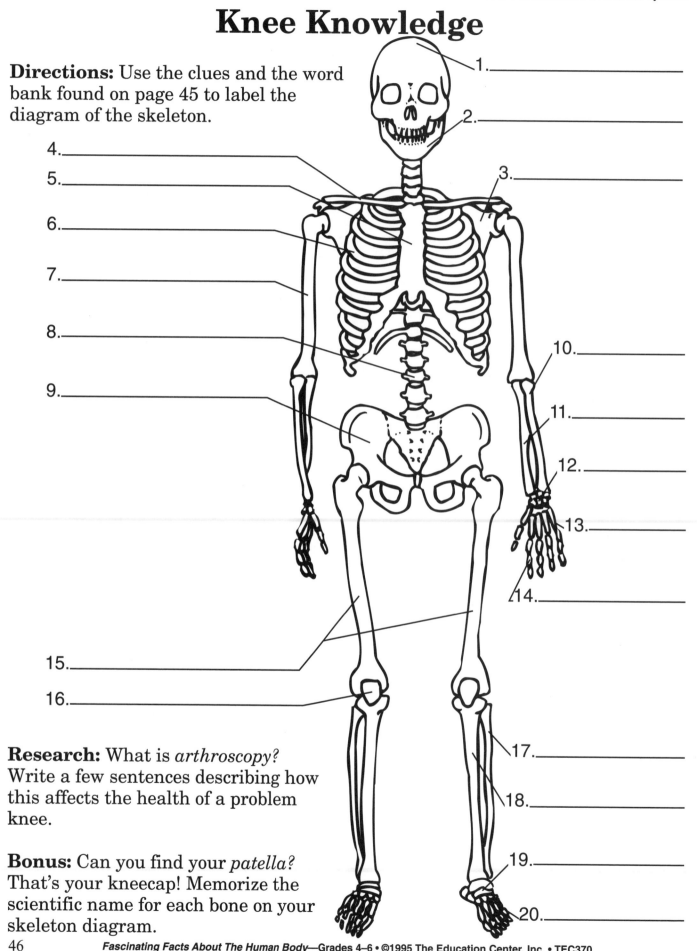

Directions: Use the clues and the word bank found on page 45 to label the diagram of the skeleton.

1._____

2._____

3._____

4._____

5._____

6._____

7._____

8._____

9._____

10._____

11._____

12._____

13._____

14._____

15._____

16._____

17._____

18._____

19._____

20._____

Research: What is *arthroscopy?* Write a few sentences describing how this affects the health of a problem knee.

Bonus: Can you find your *patella?* That's your kneecap! Memorize the scientific name for each bone on your skeleton diagram.

The Excellent Elbow

Your *funny bone* isn't really a bone at all. It's a spot on your elbow.

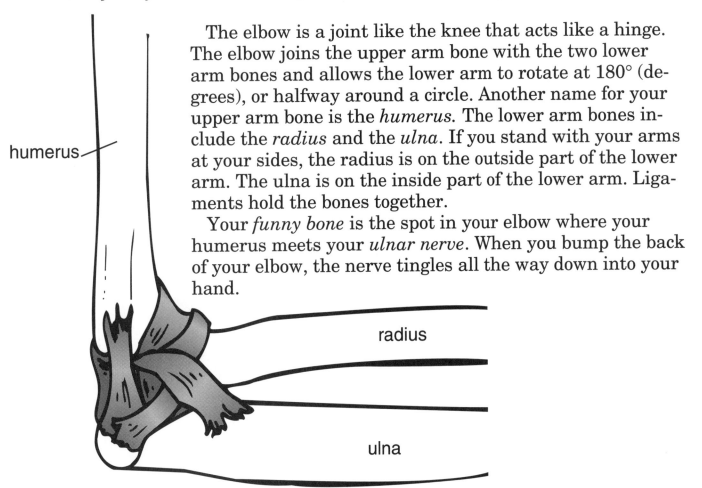

The elbow is a joint like the knee that acts like a hinge. The elbow joins the upper arm bone with the two lower arm bones and allows the lower arm to rotate at 180° (degrees), or halfway around a circle. Another name for your upper arm bone is the *humerus*. The lower arm bones include the *radius* and the *ulna*. If you stand with your arms at your sides, the radius is on the outside part of the lower arm. The ulna is on the inside part of the lower arm. Ligaments hold the bones together.

Your *funny bone* is the spot in your elbow where your humerus meets your *ulnar nerve*. When you bump the back of your elbow, the nerve tingles all the way down into your hand.

Directions: Use a complete sentence to answer each question.

1. Describe the elbow joint.

_____

2. What is the humerus?

_____

3. What are the radius and the ulna?

_____

4. Does bumping your funny bone make you smile? Why or why not?

_____

The Excellent Elbow

Directions: Use the clues to complete the crossword puzzle.

Across:
4. These hold bones together.
6. to move in a circle
7. one of the lower arm bones
8. measurement for how far things rotate

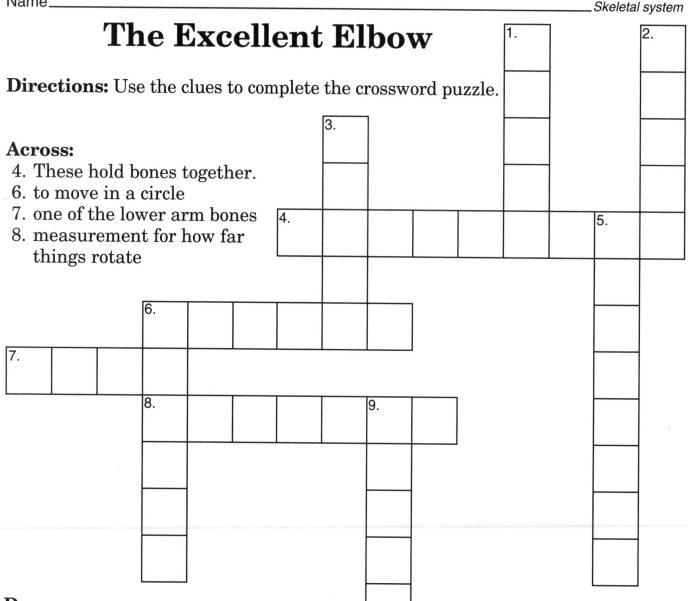

Down:
1. The elbow joint acts like this.
2. what the elbow does with upper and lower arm bones
3. connects two bones
5. Ligaments hold bones _____ .
6. another lower arm bone
9. joint featured in the text

Research: Draw a circle. Use a compass if you have one. A circle is 360° around. Divide the circle in half. That makes 180° on each side of the circle. Divide one of the halves in half. That's 90°. Rotate your head from side to side. How many degrees do you think your neck can move your head? Be natural. Don't force it. Next hold your leg still with both hands. Rotate your foot. Approximately how many degrees will it rotate? Experiment with other joints.

Bonus: What is a *lever*? Draw a picture on the back to show how the elbow works as a lever.

Shifting The Shoulder

Your shoulder is the only joint in your body that can rotate 360 degrees.

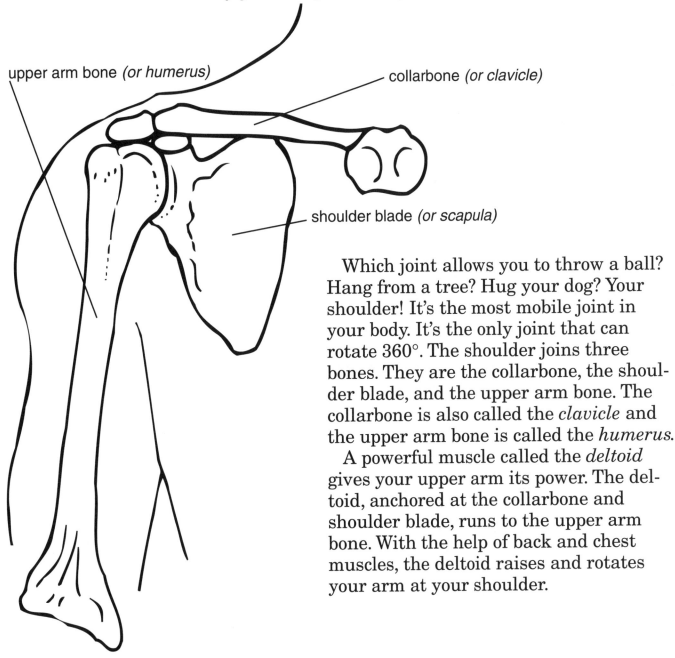

upper arm bone *(or humerus)*

collarbone *(or clavicle)*

shoulder blade *(or scapula)*

Which joint allows you to throw a ball? Hang from a tree? Hug your dog? Your shoulder! It's the most mobile joint in your body. It's the only joint that can rotate 360°. The shoulder joins three bones. They are the collarbone, the shoulder blade, and the upper arm bone. The collarbone is also called the *clavicle* and the upper arm bone is called the *humerus*.

A powerful muscle called the *deltoid* gives your upper arm its power. The deltoid, anchored at the collarbone and shoulder blade, runs to the upper arm bone. With the help of back and chest muscles, the deltoid raises and rotates your arm at your shoulder.

Directions: Write T for true or F for false before each statement.

_____ 1. Your shoulder is the most mobile joint in your body.

_____ 2. The deltoid is an upper arm bone.

_____ 3. The shoulder can rotate in a complete circle.

_____ 4. Your collarbone is your clavicle.

Shifting The Shoulder

Directions: Use the words in the text to complete the crossword puzzles.

Clues:

1. the upper arm bone
2. another name for the clavicle
3. what the text is about
4. powerful muscle
5. Your shoulder joins_____ bones.
6. Your shoulder can rotate 360 _____.

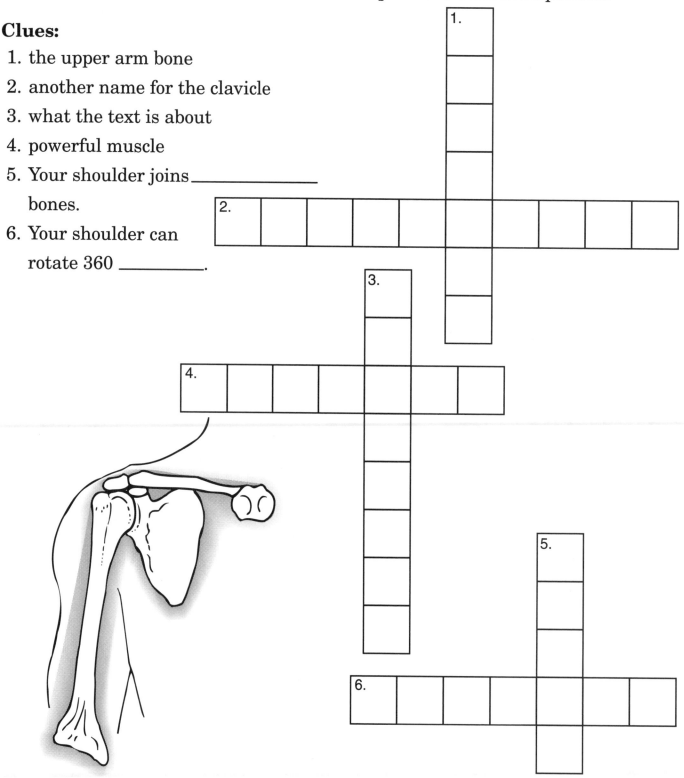

Research: What is a *rotator cuff?* In a few sentences, describe it.

Bonus: Use your deltoids! List five things you can do with your deltoid muscles.

Fascinating Facts About The Human Body—Grades 4–6 • ©1995 The Education Center, Inc. • TEC370

The Long Bones

Scientists can look at the bones of a dead person and correctly guess the sex of the skeleton 98% of the time.

Bones are actually living parts of you. Less than 50% of a bone is hard. 25% of it is water. The rest is living cells and tissue.

The bones in your arms and legs are called the *long bones.* Long bones raise and lower like levers. Your biggest long bone is your thighbone or *femur.* Inside this long bone is a yellow marrow that contains fat. On the end of the bone is a spongy area with space where nerves and blood vessels run in and out. This space is filled with red marrow.

A woman's bones are usually smaller and more delicate than a man's.

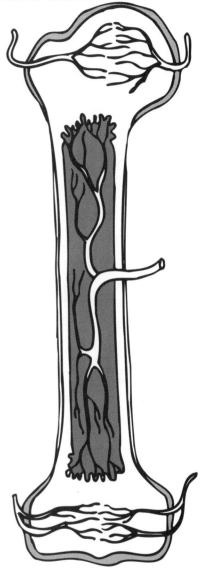

Directions: Use a complete sentence to answer each question.

1. Describe the ends of your bones. _____
_____

2. What percentage of a bone is water, hard material, and living cells? _____
_____

3. How are the bones of a woman different from the bones of a man? _____
_____

The Long Bones

Directions: Use the text to label the long bones.

1. The **humerus** is connected to your shoulder.
2. The **radius** is the outside arm bone below the elbow.
3. The **ulna** is the inside arm bone below the elbow.
4. Your biggest bone is your thighbone or **femur.**
5. The **fibula** is the outside leg bone below the knee.
6. The **tibia** or shin bone is the largest bone below the knee.

1. _____

2. _____

3. _____

4. _____

5. _____

6. _____

Research: A girl usually has a longer forefinger than ring finger. For a boy, the ring finger is usually longer. Take a class poll. How many girls have ring fingers longer than their forefingers? How many boys? Write a fraction to show the results of each poll.

Bonus: Trace your hand on the back of this paper. Label your ring finger, forefinger, and thumb. Draw a ring on your ring finger.

Body Cushions

**When you were born, much of your skeleton was still cartilage.
As you grew, it turned to bone.**

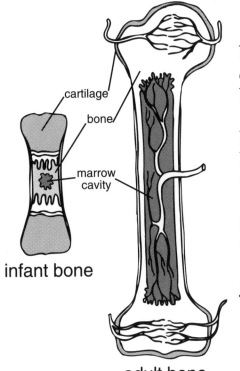

cartilage

bone

marrow
cavity

infant bone

adult bone

What does a cushion feel like? It's soft and comes between you and something hard, like the seat of a chair. Cushioning is what *cartilage* does for your bones.

Cartilage is soft tissue found at the ends of bones. Cartilage is more slippery than ice. It allows bones to move against one another without causing damage.

The cartilage we hear the most about is in the knee. You can feel cartilage at the end of your nose or in your outer ear. Can you imagine what it would be like to not have cartilage cushioning the joints of your bones?

Directions: Use a complete sentence to answer each question.

1. What does cartilage do for your bones?

_____

_____

2. Describe cartilage.

_____

_____

3. Describe your bones at birth.

_____

_____

Body Cushions

Directions: To learn something else about cartilage, use the number code to decode the message.

A = 1	B = 2	C = 3	D = 4	E = 5	F = 6	G = 7
H = 8	I = 9	J = 10	K = 11	L = 12	M = 13	N = 14
O = 15	P = 16	Q = 17	R = 18	S = 19	T = 20	U = 21
V = 22	W = 23	X = 24	Y = 25	Z = 26		

‾ ‾ ‾ ‾ ‾ ‾ ‾ ‾ ‾   ‾ ‾   ‾ ‾ ‾ ‾ ‾ ‾ ‾ ‾   ‾ ‾ ‾
3, 1, 18, 20, 9, 12, 1, 7, 5   9, 19   6, 12, 5, 24, 9, 2, 12, 5   1, 14, 4

‾ ‾ ‾ ‾ ‾   ‾ ‾ ‾ ‾   ‾ ‾ ‾ ‾ ‾   ‾ ‾ ‾
7, 9, 22, 5, 19   23, 8, 5, 14   2, 15, 14, 5, 19   1, 18, 5

‾ ‾ ‾ ‾ ‾ ‾   ‾ ‾   ‾ ‾   ‾ ‾ ‾ ‾ ‾
10, 1, 18, 18, 5, 4   19, 15   9, 20   13, 1, 11, 5, 19

‾   ‾ ‾ ‾ ‾   ‾ ‾ ‾ ‾ ‾   ‾ ‾ ‾ ‾ ‾ ‾ ‾ ‾.
1   7, 15, 15, 4   19, 8, 15, 3, 11   1, 2, 19, 15, 18, 2, 5, 18

Research: Look up *friction*. Why don't we want friction between our bones? What would happen if our bones didn't have cartilage?

Bonus: Find some objects that you think are like cushions (a sponge, a scrap of foam rubber, or a piece of rubber band). How many others can you find? Find some hard objects. You need two of each. Objects you may use are blocks, dominoes, dice, or stones. Rub the two hard objects together. Then put a cushion between them. How does a cushion change the way the hard objects move against each other?

Joining With Joints

Bones squeak in old age because the lubricating fluid between the bones dries up.

Joints are where bones are linked together. There are different kinds of joints. *Fixed joints* do not move. Joints connecting bones in the skull are examples of fixed joints. *Hinge joints* allow movement in one direction. The elbow and knee joints move like hinges. *Ball-and-socket joints* allow the bones to swing in almost any direction. These joints also allow the bones to twist. The shoulder joint is an example of a ball-and-socket joint.

A joint where one bone rests and rotates from a particular point is called a *pivotal joint*. Your head rests on a pivotal joint. The joint where two bones that can move separately meet is called a *sliding* or *gliding joint*. Your arm and hand can both move in separate directions or in the same direction at once. Your wrist is an example of a sliding joint.

Directions: Label each joint shown: pivotal, hinge, ball-and-socket, and sliding/gliding.

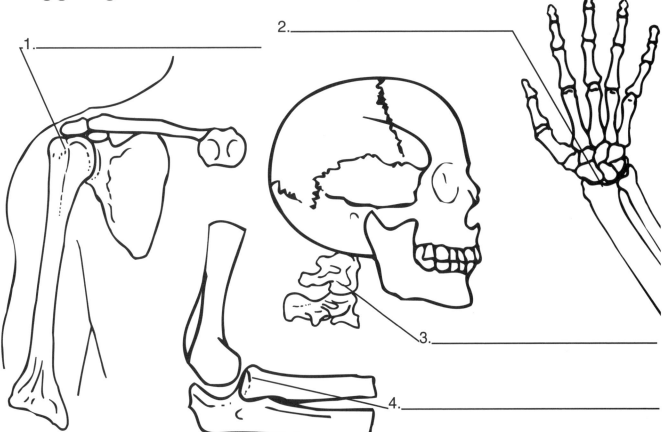

1._____

2._____

3._____

4._____

Joining With Joints

Directions: Hidden in the word-search puzzle are ten words from the text. The words are written vertically, horizontally, and diagonally. How many of the ten can you find? There may be other words in the puzzle that are not in the text, but they don't count. Find and circle only words from the text.

l	b	o	n	e	s	i	s	t
w	i	h	i	p	v	r	w	f
r	w	n	p	l	z	m	i	i
i	p	s	k	u	l	l	v	x
s	y	a	g	e	q	g	e	e
t	l	m	t	o	d	b	l	d
h	i	n	g	e	m	d	j	f
k	n	s	w	i	n	g	h	q
j	k	f	k	t	w	i	s	t

Research: *Arthritis* is a disease that affects joints. Find out about arthritis and write a few sentences about it.

Bonus: Choose ten different words from the text and create your own word-search puzzle. Give it to a friend to solve.

Connecting Muscle And Bone

What helps you stand on your toes and walk up and down stairs? Your *Achilles tendon*.

Tendons are long, fibrous cords that connect muscles and bones. The Achilles tendon is located in the back of your ankle. It is the largest tendon in your body. The Achilles tendon connects your calf muscles with your heel bones.

Without tendons you would not be able to move. You have tendons in each of your fingers and toes. The muscles that move your fingers are located in your lower arms. The tendons in your arms and fingers help you move them. The muscles that move your toes are in each calf (the lower leg).

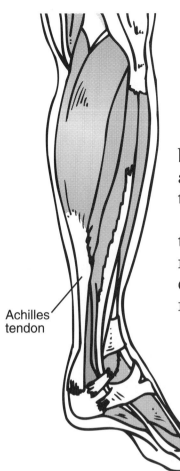

Achilles tendon

Directions: Use the number code to label and color the diagram of some of the bones in your hand and foot.

1. The **carpals** are the bones in your wrist. Color them green.
2. The **ulna** is always the bone on the little-finger side. Color it purple.
3. The **radius** is always the bone on the thumb side. Color it red.
4. The **phalanges** are finger and toe bones. Color them yellow.
5. The **tarsals** are the ankle bones. Color them blue.
6. The **fibula** is the outer bone of the lower leg. Color it brown.
7. The **tibia** (shinbone) is the inner bone of the lower leg. Color it orange.

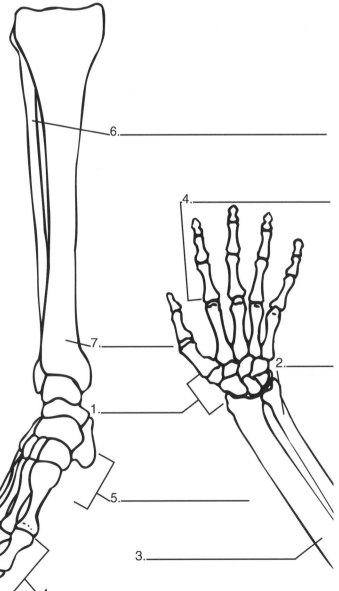

Connecting Muscle And Bone

Directions: Use the clues to solve the crossword puzzle.

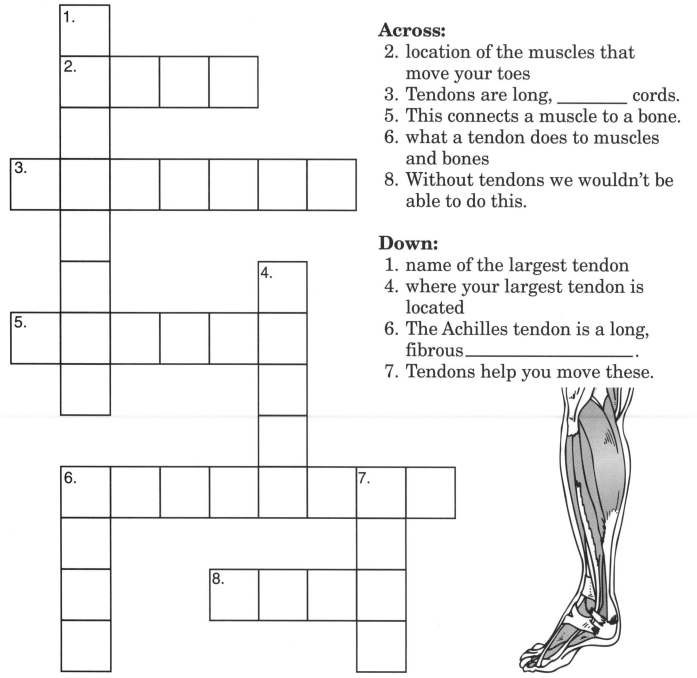

Across:
2. location of the muscles that move your toes
3. Tendons are long, _____ cords.
5. This connects a muscle to a bone.
6. what a tendon does to muscles and bones
8. Without tendons we wouldn't be able to do this.

Down:
1. name of the largest tendon
4. where your largest tendon is located
6. The Achilles tendon is a long, fibrous _____ .
7. Tendons help you move these.

Research: Muscles get their energy from *glucose,* which comes from the carbohydrates you eat. Find out which foods are carbohydrates. Make a list of at least 15 carbohydrate foods.

Bonus: Pretend you are a string puppet or a *marionette* without tendons, muscles, and bones. Imagine the puppeteer pulling your strings. Then imagine that a fairy uses magic to turn you into a real boy or girl. Write a paragraph that tells how it feels to have muscles that work.

Every Time You Move

Every time you move, you move a muscle. There are about 650 muscles in your body.

The biggest and one of the most powerful muscles is the *gluteus maximus* in each *buttock*. Your smallest muscles are in your ear.

Some muscles (like those in your arms and legs) work only when you want them to. Other muscles (like those in your heart and intestines) work automatically. *Tendons* join muscles to bones. If you don't use your muscles, they will get weak.

Directions: Use the number code to label and color the **front** view of the muscular system.

1. The **deltoid** is a large muscle covering the joint of the shoulder. Color it blue.
2. **Pectoral muscles** are the two muscles on either side of the chest wall. Color them red.
3. The **biceps** are the muscles in the upper arm. Color them purple.
4. The **rectus abdominis** muscles are the straight muscles of the abdomen and thigh. Color them yellow.
5. The **sartorius** is a long, flat, narrow muscle extending from the front of the hip to the inner side of the leg. Color it orange.
6. The **quadriceps**, a large, four-part muscle at the front of the thigh, extends the leg or bends it at the hip joint. Color it green.
7. The **gastrocnemius** is the largest muscle in the calf of the leg. Color it brown.

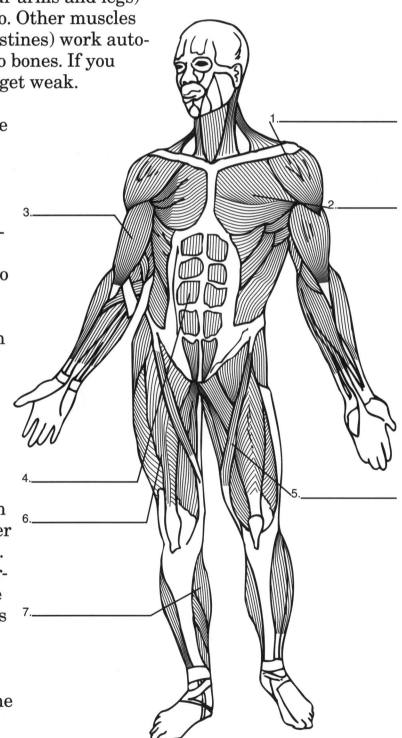

Every Time You Move

Directions: Use the number code to label and color the diagram of the **back** view of the muscular system.

1. The **trapezius** is a broad, flat muscle on each side of the upper back. Color it red.
2. The **deltoid** is a large, triangular muscle covering the joint of the shoulder. Color it blue.
3. The **triceps** are muscles at the back of the upper arm. Color them yellow.
4. The **latissimus dorsi** is a broad, flat muscle on each side of the middle of the back. Color it purple.
5. The **gluteus maximus** is the broad, thick, outermost muscle on each buttock. Color it green.
6. The **gastrocnemius** is the largest muscle in the calf of the leg. Color it brown.

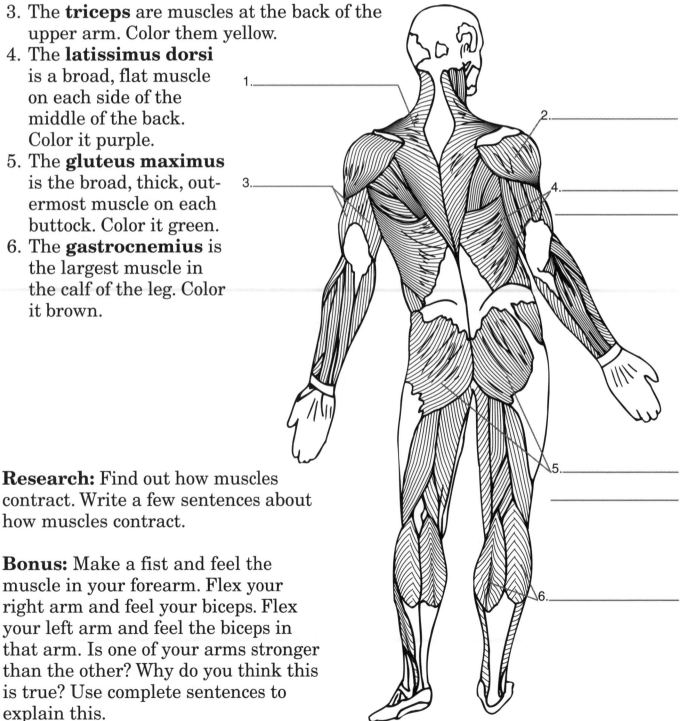

Research: Find out how muscles contract. Write a few sentences about how muscles contract.

Bonus: Make a fist and feel the muscle in your forearm. Flex your right arm and feel your biceps. Flex your left arm and feel the biceps in that arm. Is one of your arms stronger than the other? Why do you think this is true? Use complete sentences to explain this.

 Fascinating Facts About The Human Body—Grades 4–6 • ©1995 The Education Center, Inc. • TEC370

The Beautiful Brain

Neurons of a fetus or baby before birth form at the rate of about 250,000 per minute.

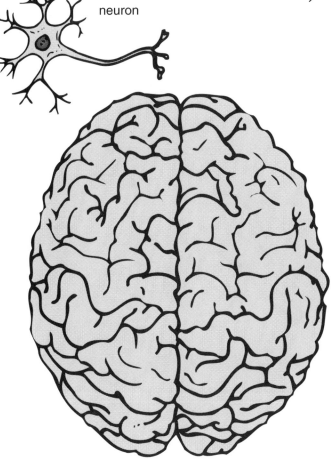

neuron

Are you thinking? Your brain is at work. Are you daydreaming? Your brain is still working. Will you be sleeping soon? Your brain will be at work then too. Your brain never rests. Your brain is the most complex part of your nervous system.

Although your brain makes up only about 2% of your body's weight, it consumes 20% of the energy your body produces. You get this energy from glucose and oxygen carried to the brain in the bloodstream. The brain controls all of your thoughts and movements. The average human brain weighs about three pounds. It is filled with a jellylike substance. The brain consists of 100 billion nerve cells called *neurons*. Neurons carry the brain's messages, or nerve signals, to other parts of the body.

Directions: Write T for true or F for false before each sentence.

_____ 1. When you think, your brain is at rest.

_____ 2. When you daydream, your brain is working.

_____ 3. When you sleep, your brain stops working.

_____ 4. Your brain controls every thought that you have.

_____ 5. Your brain controls all of your movements.

_____ 6. The average human brain weighs about three ounces.

_____ 7. Your brain contains a substance like jelly.

_____ 8. Your brain consists of billions of nerve cells.

_____ 9. Neurons carry food and nutrients to other parts of the body.

_____10. Neurons carry messages and signals from the brain.

The Beautiful Brain

Directions: Use the number code to label and color the diagram of the brain.

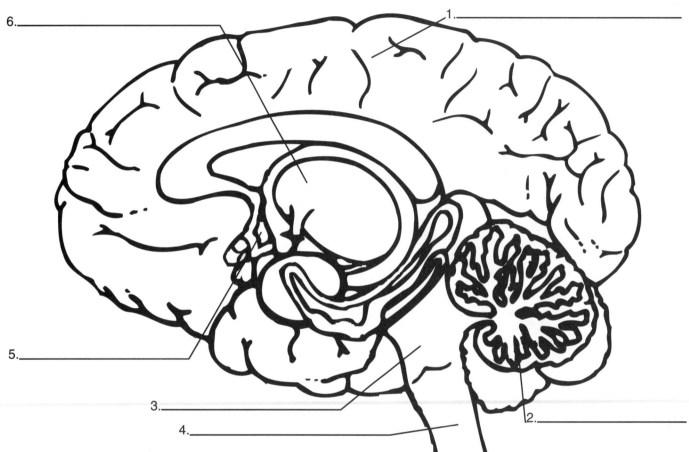

1. The intelligence center of the brain is called the **cerebrum**. It controls memory, thinking, and learning. It also receives and interprets messages from the five senses. Color it pink.
2. The **cerebellum** controls muscular coordination and balance. Color it red.
3. The **medulla** controls involuntary functions such as breathing, heartbeat, and digestion. Color it yellow.
4. The **spinal cord** is the large nerve leading from the brain and extending down the back. Color it green.
5. The **hypothalamus** is the control center for appetite, water balance, sleepiness, and temperature control. Color it purple.
6. The **thalamus** is the center of your feelings such as anger, pleasure, and basic drives. Color it orange.

Research: Find out what the difference is between right-brain activities and left-brain activities. Write a few sentences about this.

Bonus: List the six parts of the brain. Then write an action that each part of your brain controls. Example: cerebellum—walking, thalamus—laughing.

Brainy Bonanza

You have about 100 billion neurons in your brain. That's about as many stars as there are in our galaxy.

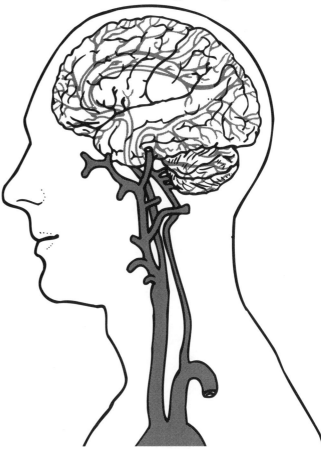

Your brain can think, plan, and study things. Your brain can even think and learn about itself. What does your brain need? Blood is very important to your brain. If blood circulation to the brain is stopped, brain tissue may die. If blood circulation to the brain is disturbed in any way, hearing, sight, feeling, or movement may be affected.

The brain is a complex body part. It is a hungry one, too. Even though your brain is relatively small, it requires 20% of your heart's freshly oxygenated blood supply. And your brain uses 20% of the blood's important nutrients—oxygen and glucose.

Directions: Circle the letter of the best answer for each question.

1. What percentage of fresh blood does the brain use?

   (a) 10%   (b) 20%   (c) 50%

2. How much of the blood's oxygen supply does your brain use?

   (a) 10%   (b) 20%   (c) 50%

3. As a body part, your brain is

   (a) complex   (b) relatively small   (c) both a and b

4. Which one is an important nutrient for the brain?

   (a) oxygen   (b) glucose   (c) both a and b

Brainy Bonanza

Directions: Use the clues to complete the crossword puzzle.

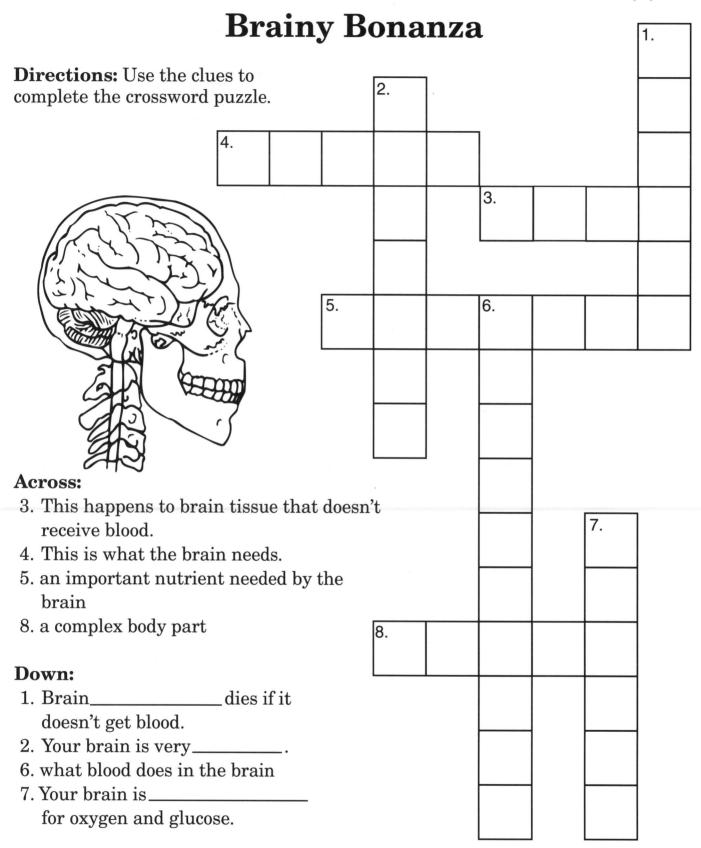

Across:
3. This happens to brain tissue that doesn't receive blood.
4. This is what the brain needs.
5. an important nutrient needed by the brain
8. a complex body part

Down:
1. Brain_____ dies if it doesn't get blood.
2. Your brain is very_____ .
6. what blood does in the brain
7. Your brain is_____ for oxygen and glucose.

Research: What is the *hypothalamus?* In a few sentences, describe what it does.

Bonus: Find out how long your brain can live without oxygen. What does it mean when a patient is *brain-dead?*

What's On Top?

It takes about 12 muscles to frown but only 10 to smile!

Your skull protects an amazing brain that is like a huge computer, controlling everything your body does. Many muscles attach the base of the skull to bones in the upper chest and to the vertebrae and shoulder blades. These muscles allow you to balance and move your head on the topmost bones of your spine. About 30 muscles in your head allow you to make all your facial expressions. Your head houses your brain and your sensory receptors: the eyes, ears, nose, and mouth.

Directions: Use the number code to label and color the diagram of the head found on page 66.

1. Your **eyes** transmit images to the brain and this gives you vision. Color the eye pink.
2. The **nasal passage** warms the air you breathe and carries aromas to sensory cells. Color it yellow.
3. The **tongue** tastes food and sends the flavor message to the brain. Color it purple.
4. The **spinal cord** relays information from the nerves to the brain. Color it green.
5. The **center for smell and taste** is where the brain processes messages about aromas and flavors. Color it orange.
6. The **center for vision** is where the brain processes messages about sight. Color it blue.

Research: Find out how big the brains of some animals are. Compare the size of their brains to the size of their bodies. Compare the size of the human brain to the human body size. Write a few statements about this.

Bonus: Put a large piece of paper on the floor. Get a friend to lie on the paper, then draw around his/her body. Now add the systems that you have been studying. Can you draw the heart, blood vessels, backbone, arm and leg bones, etc. ? How many body parts can you accurately add and label on your illustration?

What's On Top?

Directions: Use the number code found on page 65 to label and color the diagram of the head.

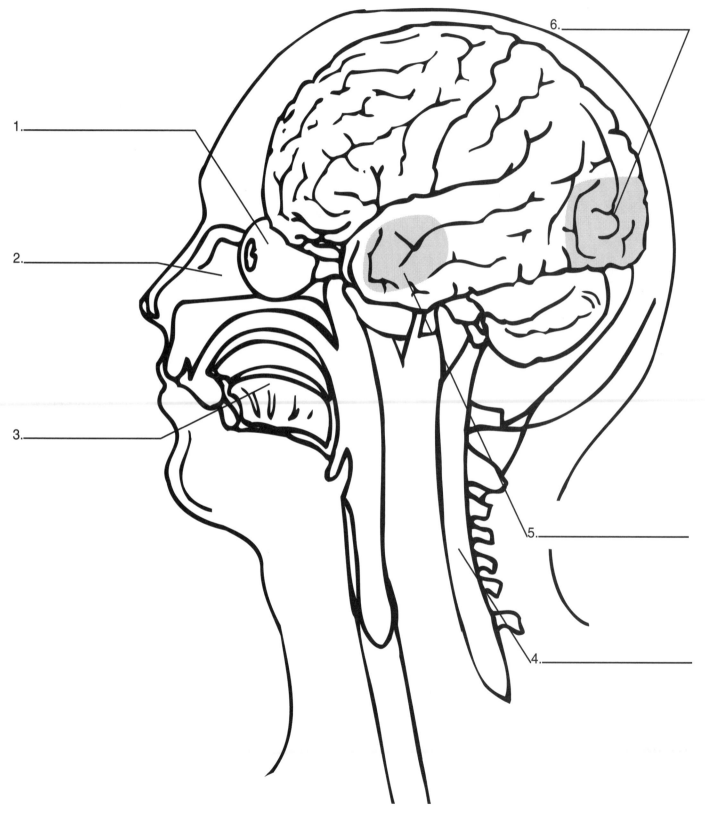

Spinal Signals

Nerves in your spinal cord can pass messages along to your brain and muscles as fast as 350 feet per second. That's almost 250 miles per hour!

The *spinal cord* is a bundle of nerves that runs down the *spinal column*. These nerves run through a series of holes in the vertebrae. The spinal cord goes from the brain to the bottom of the spine. Between the vertebrae, there are gaps. Through these gaps, 31 pairs of nerves enter and leave the spinal cord. The spinal cord carries messages and signals back and forth.

Think of your spinal cord as a great nerve highway linking the brain to the rest of your body. If you touch a hot stove, the nerves in your fingers will send a message to the nerves in your spinal cord. The nerves in your spinal cord forward the message to your brain. It tells you what you have done and tells your arm muscles to jerk your hand away. It is a good thing the nerves can pass messages along to your brain at great speeds.

Directions: Unscramble the words to complete the sentences.

1. The (a p s i n l) _____ cord is a (e n u b d l) _____

   of (v r n e s e) _____.

2. The spinal (d c r o) _____ runs down the spinal

   (l c n o m u) _____.

3. The spinal cord runs through a series of (e s o h l) _____

   in the (r v t e e r b e a) _____.

4. The spinal cord goes from the (n b a i r) _____ to the bottom of

   the (e s n i p) _____.

Spinal Signals

Directions: Use the number code to label and color the diagram of the nervous system. Use colored pencils or pens for this activity.

1. Your **brain** sits at the top of the spinal cord. Color it yellow.
2. The **spinal cord** is the cord of nerve tissue extending through the spinal canal of the spinal column. Color the spinal column purple.
3. **Nerves** run **along the arms** and signal the brain when you want to move your arms. Color the nerves along the arms orange.
4. There are a lot of **automatic nerves** that go to each organ. Color these nerves green.
5. **Nerves** also run **along the legs** and signal the brain when you want to move your legs. Color the nerves along the legs orange, also.

1. _____

2. _____

3. _____

4. _____

5. _____

Research: Look up *neurons*. Draw a picture of two neurons touching. Label the *synapse*.

Bonus: What does it mean to be *a bundle of nerves?* Describe three *nerve-wracking* situations you have had.

You Get Under My Skin!

An adult's skin weighs about ten pounds.

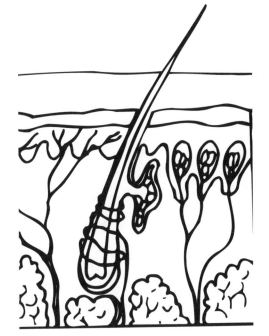

Your skin is a watertight container that prevents your internal sea from gushing, or drying up. Skin is composed of two layers. The thin, tough, top layer is the *epidermis*. Cells at the bottom of the epidermis are always dividing and producing new cells. As old cells die, they are pushed to the top by the new cells. It takes about a month for a new cell to travel from the bottom to the top of this layer of skin.

Have you noticed when you get a cut how long it takes to form a scab and then heal? How long does it take for the scar to disappear? Your skin renews itself. If it didn't, every cut and scrape that you get would leave a mark on your skin.

Directions: Your skin is very complex. Skin prints are unique for each person. Fingerprints are a way of identifying people. Use an ink pad to make fingerprints and thumbprints in the box. Label each print you make.

You Get Under My Skin!

Directions: To complete this activity, you will need a partner and the following items: 1 blindfold, 3 lemons (different sizes), 3 bananas (different sizes), 2 apples, 1 pair of cotton gloves, and 1 pair of rubber gloves. Sit blindfolded as your partner reads each exercise and hands you the appropriate items. Then blindfold your partner and repeat the activity.

_____ 1. Wearing rubber gloves, can you tell which lemon is the largest?

_____ 2. Wearing the cloth gloves, can you tell which banana is the longest?

_____ 3. Wearing no gloves, feel one lemon. Then have your partner hand you all three lemons. Can you find the first lemon you touched?

_____ 4. Wearing no gloves, feel one banana. Then have your partner hand you all three bananas. Can you find the first banana you touched?

_____ 5. Wearing cloth gloves, can you distinguish and sort lemons from apples?

_____ 6. Wearing rubber gloves, can you distinguish and sort lemons from apples?

_____ 7. Wearing no gloves, can you distinguish and sort lemons from apples?

_____ 8. Wearing cloth gloves, can you distinguish the top of an apple from the bottom?

Research: Get some fruit "skins" like orange, apple, and banana peels. Get some potato, turnip, and carrot "skins" too. On which of these do we find the thinnest skin? The thickest? On our bodies, where is the thinnest skin? Why do you think it is thinner in some places than in others? Write a paragraph on your observations about skins.

Bonus: Look up *melanin*. In a few sentences, describe melanin.

The Second Layer

In certain places, one square inch of your skin has over 650 sweat glands!

The top layer of your skin protects you from water, dust, and germs. Under the top layer, called the *epidermis,* there is another layer. This much thicker layer is called the *dermis.* The dermis contains supportive tissue, hair follicles, nerves, blood vessels, and millions of tiny sweat glands. Your sweat glands help regulate your body's temperature. They produce a watery liquid called *perspiration.* Perspiration cools you off when you get too hot.

Your skin is also a storehouse for fats and glycogen (stored glucose). When stimulated by sunlight, your skin can make vitamin D. It can also absorb medicines applied to its surface.

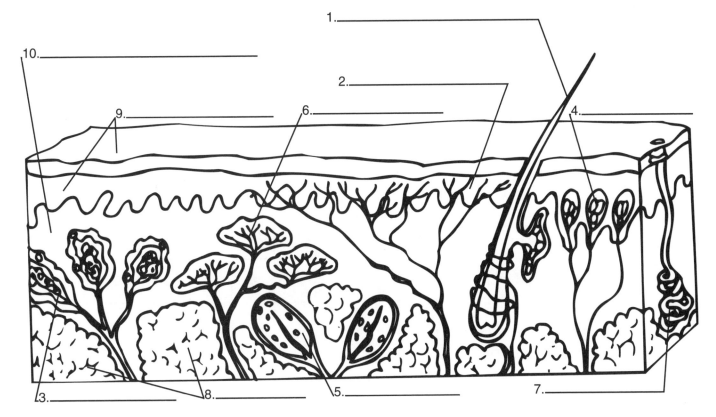

Directions: Use the number code to label and color each part of the diagram of your skin.

1. Color the **hair** black.
2. Color **pain receptors** orange.
3. Color **cold receptors** blue.
4. Color **touch receptors** green.
5. Color **pressure receptors** yellow.
6. Color **heat receptors** red.
7. Color the **sweat gland** purple.
8. Color **fat** gray.
9. Color the **epidermis** pink.
10. Color the **dermis** brown.

The Second Layer

Directions: Use the clues to solve the crossword puzzle.

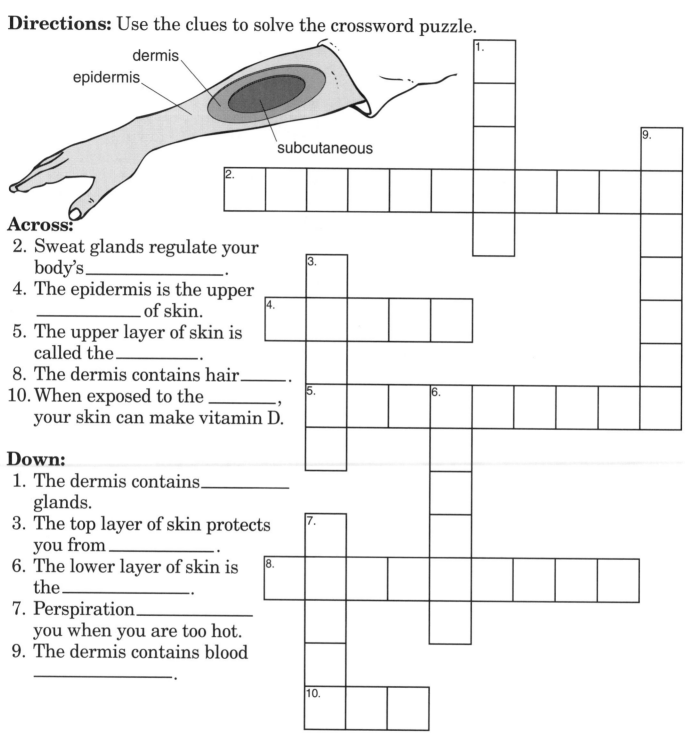

dermis
epidermis
subcutaneous

Across:

2. Sweat glands regulate your body's_____.
4. The epidermis is the upper _____ of skin.
5. The upper layer of skin is called the_____.
8. The dermis contains hair_____.
10. When exposed to the _____, your skin can make vitamin D.

Down:

1. The dermis contains_____ glands.
3. The top layer of skin protects you from_____.
6. The lower layer of skin is the_____.
7. Perspiration_____ you when you are too hot.
9. The dermis contains blood _____.

Research: Some animals can change the color of their skin. List three animals that can camouflage themselves by changing colors.

Bonus: Go to the library and look up *skin*. Draw a picture of the *dermis* and the *epidermis*. Color the two parts different colors. Write two characteristics of each layer on your diagram. Label each part and color the label the same color as you colored that layer of skin.

Knowing About Nails

If you never cut or break your nails, they might grow to be as long as three feet!

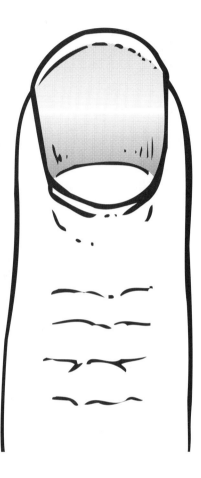

Hair and nails are dead structures made of *keratin*. Keratin is a kind of protein that protects and waterproofs the outer layer of your skin. Fingernails give your fingers support as you handle or touch objects. They allow you to do delicate things such as untie a knot.

Did you know that your fingernails grow about 0.004 inch a day—which is about 0.12 inch a month or about 1 1/2 inches a year? Have you ever noticed that your fingernails grow about three times as fast as your toenails? The nails on the longest fingers grow the fastest. If you are right-handed, the nails on your right hand grow faster than the nails on your left hand.

Hair and nails have no nerve endings, and that is why cutting them doesn't hurt. Underneath the white area at the base of the nail is a layer of cells from which the nail grows. Damage to this white "half-moon" can cause the nail to stop growing.

Directions: Unscramble the words to complete each sentence.

1. Hair and nails are made of (r a k t n i e)_____.

2. Keratin is a (n r p o t i e) _____.

3. Fingernails grow about 1 1/2 (h s n i c e)_____ each year.

Knowing About Nails

Directions: Write T for true or F for false before each sentence.

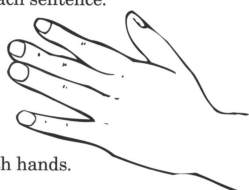

_____ 1. Fingernails grow faster than toenails.

_____ 2. All fingernails grow at the same speed.

_____ 3. Fingernails grow at the same speed on both hands.

_____ 4. Fingernails and hair are made of the same substance.

_____ 5. The nails on the shortest fingers grow the fastest.

_____ 6. Fingernails help you do delicate things like tie a bow.

_____ 7. Hair and nails are dead.

_____ 8. Nails on your toes grow faster than nails on your hands.

_____ 9. Nails have no nerve endings.

_____ 10. The cells under the white area at the base of the nail are dead.

Research: What is *keratin?* Write a few sentences describing keratin.

Bonus: Draw a picture of your dominant hand. Measure your fingernails, and make the fingernails you draw exactly the same size as the nails on your fingers. Next cut a strip of paper one inch wide and three feet long, and tape it to one fingernail. That is how long your nails could be if you didn't cut or break them. What does it feel like? If your fingernails were really that long all the time, how would that affect your daily activities?

I Only Have Eyes For You!

**Did you know that you blink every two to ten seconds?
Can you not blink for a whole minute? Try it!**

The eye is shaped like a ball. It has muscles attached to it so it can move up and down and from side to side. The front part of the eye is called the *cornea*. Behind the cornea is the *iris*, a colored ring of muscles. The iris surrounds the *pupil*. The pupil gets smaller in bright light and larger in dim light. This regulates the amount of light sent to the delicate *retina* at the back of the eye. Light bounces off what you see and enters the eye through the pupil. Nerves in the retina send messages to the brain.

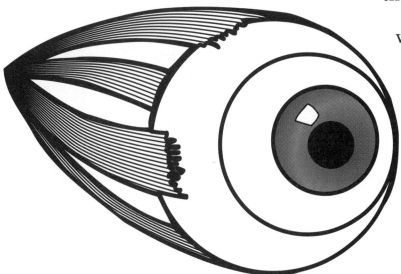

The brain tells you what you see. Besides shapes and sizes, your eyes tell you what color things are. However, about 1 in every 20 people cannot see colors properly. When a person cannot distinguish colors, he is said to be color-blind.

Directions: Use the number code to label and color the diagram of the eye found on page 76.

1. Color the **cornea** light blue.
2. Color the **lens** dark blue.
3. Color the **iris** black.
4. Color the **fluids** red.
5. Color the **retina** brown.
6. Color the **muscles** orange.
7. Color the **optic nerve** purple.
8. Color the **blind spot** green.

I Only Have Eyes For You!

Directions: Use the number code on page 75 to label and color the diagram of the eye.

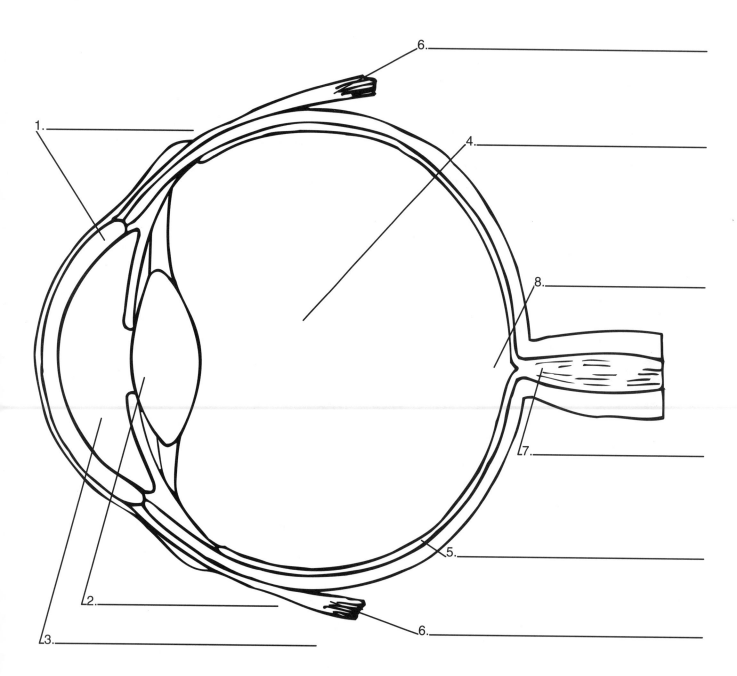

Research: As people age, their eyes change and they may need *bifocal lenses.* What is a bifocal lens? Do you know someone who wears bifocals? Ask him why he wears them. In a few sentences, describe what bifocal lenses do.

Bonus: Find out what eyes and cameras have in common. In a paragraph describe how they are similar and how they are different.

Now Hear This!

The three bones of the middle ear—hammer, anvil, and stirrup—are so small that all three could easily fit on your fingernail.

The ear is made up of three parts: the outer ear, the middle ear, and the inner ear. You can see only the outer ear. The rest is inside your head. Air movements, called sound waves, enter the outer ear. The sound wave travels inside and makes the eardrum, in the middle ear, vibrate. The inner ear turns the vibrations into nerve impulses that are sent to the brain. The brain tells you what you hear. The inner ear also helps you maintain your balance.

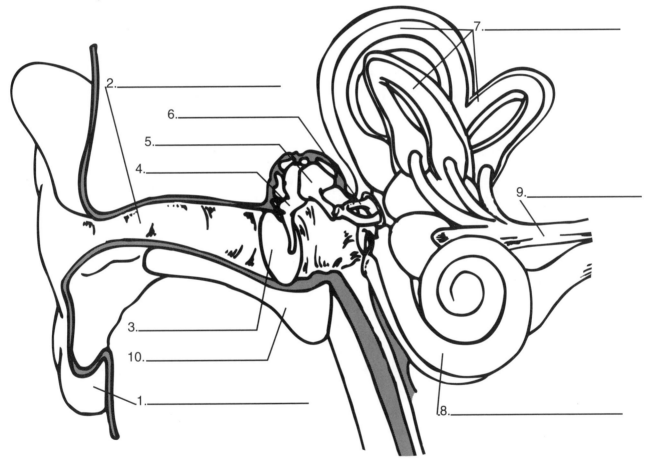

Directions: Use the number code to label and color each part of the ear.

1. Color the **auricle** blue.
2. Color the **canal** orange.
3. Color the **eardrum** purple.
4. Color the **hammer** (malleus) yellow.
5. Color the **anvil** (incus) red.
6. Color the **stirrup** (stapes) green.
7. Color the **semicircular canals** pink.
8. Color the **cochlea** brown.
9. Color the **auditory nerve** black.
10. Color the **bone** gray.

Now Hear This!

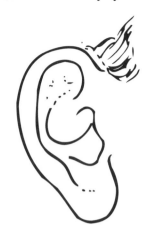

Directions: Use the clues to complete the crossword puzzles.

1. part of the ear where the eardrum is located
2. part of the ear that helps you maintain your balance
3. part of the ear that collects sound
4. part of the body that tells you what you hear
5. the kind of impulse that goes to the brain
6. part of the ear that vibrates
7. The ear helps you to maintain this.
8. what happens when sound waves hit the eardrum

Research: What is *ultrasonic sound?* In a few sentences, describe ultrasonic sound.

Bonus: Make a list of words for sounds that begin with each letter of the alphabet. Example: a—alarm, b—blast, c—crash, etc.

Name_____

The Sensing Senses

There are about 125 million light-sensitive cells called rods in the retina of your eye!

Do you know how your brain gets information about the world? Through your five senses—sight, hearing, smelling, tasting, and touching. Many feel that *sight* is the most important sense because it feeds the brain the most information about the surroundings. After sight, *hearing* is considered by some as the most important sense.

Human beings use their sense of *smell* to alert them of danger from things like smoke. Smell also helps you enjoy your food. About 80% of what you think of as taste really comes from the sense of smell.

Taste adds pleasure to your life. Your tongue has about 10,000 taste buds, each with its own nerve connection to the brain. Scientists know that the senses of taste and smell are chemical senses.

Your sense of *touch* puts you in direct contact with the world. It allows you to give and sense love. Babies who are not given human contact—not hugged or held—sometimes die just as if they weren't given food. Touch is important to keep us safe, too. When your body feels pain, it sends the message to the brain to let you know that something is wrong.

Directions: Read each sentence and fill in the blank with the sense that makes the most "sense."

1. If you close your eyes, can you_____the sunset?

2. If you are wearing gloves, can you_____velvet?

3. If you hold your nose, can you_____rotten eggs?

4. If you cover your ears, can you_____ music?

5. If you cannot smell, can you_____your food?

The Sensing Senses

Directions: The wheel is divided into five parts, one section for each sense. Notice that the brain is in the middle. In each part of the wheel, list, illustrate, or cut and paste pictures of things that you most like to sense with the appropriate sense.

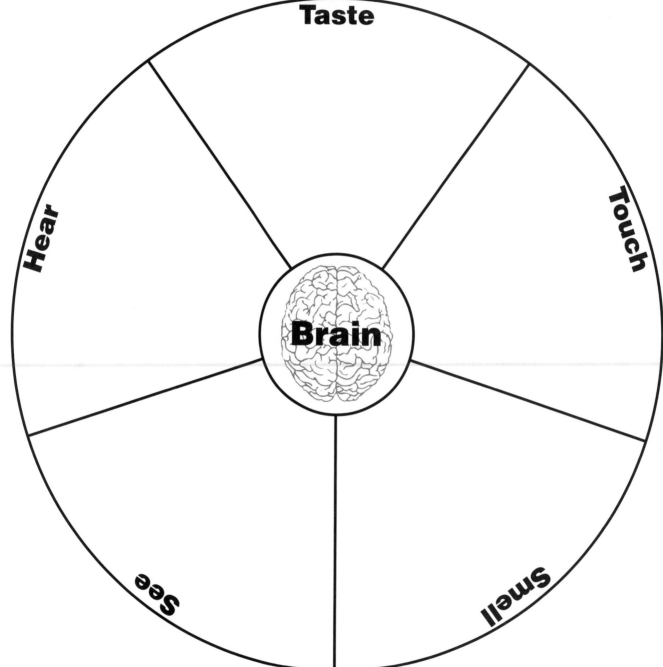

Research: What are *receptor cells?* In a few sentences, describe the role of receptor cells.

Bonus: Make another wheel like the one above, and list the things you least like to experience with each sense.

Dealing With Digestion

Did you know that digestion begins before you even begin to eat? Digestion begins when you think about eating. In anticipation, your body begins to prepare itself by producing saliva. Your mouth makes more than a quart of saliva a day.

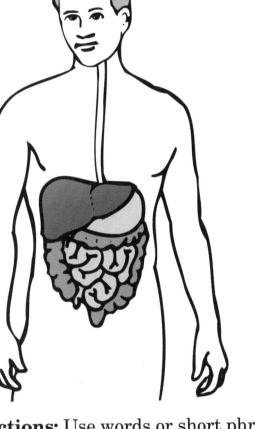

Your digestive system processes food, which provides your body with the energy it needs for maintenance and repair. When you put food into your mouth, your teeth cut, grind, crush, mash, and shred the food while mixing it with saliva. Then the food moves down a tube called the *esophagus* to the stomach. There three bands of strong muscles churn, squeeze, and break the food up into smaller pieces. An acid produced in the stomach dissolves meat and other foods.

After the food leaves the stomach, it travels through the small and large intestines, where particles of food pass through the linings of the intestines and into the blood. Powerful body chemicals called *enzymes* digest the carbohydrates, proteins, and fats that make up your diet.

Directions: Use words or short phrases to complete the sentences.

1. What is the function of the digestive system?

_____

_____

2. Name two reasons your body needs food.

_____

_____

3. Name four body parts involved in the digestive process.

_____

_____

Dealing With Digestion

Directions: Hidden in the word-search puzzle are 20 words from the text. The words are written vertically, horizontally, and diagonally. How many of them can you find? There are other words in the puzzle that are not in the text, but they don't count. Find and circle only words from the text.

```
e   s   o   p   h   a   g   u   s   c   k   h
d   t   i   n   t   e   s   t   i   n   e   s
i   o   r   g   a   n   s   f   n   e   e   z
g   m   s   y   s   t   e   m   o   u   r   b
e   a   p   b   o   d   i   e   s   o   r   r
s   c   r   e   p   a   i   r   p   l   d   e
t   h   o   n   m   o   u   t   h   i   a   a
i   f   c   e   b   b   b   r   p   n   o   t
v   a   e   r   l   a   l   o   r   i   e   c
e   t   s   g   o   n   o   t   o   n   n   o
c   s   s   y   o   d   o   e   t   g   z   n
d   i   e   t   d   k   b   i   e   s   y   e
r   i   s   f   e   t   s   n   i   m   m   s
m   a   i   n   t   e   n   a   n   c   e   p
p   a   r   t   i   c   l   e   s   q   s   e
```

Research: Find out what saliva does. Write a paragraph about it.

Bonus: What happens when your food goes down the wrong way? If someone were choking on a piece of food stuck in his windpipe, what would you do? What is the Heimlich maneuver? Draw a picture to show how it can save a life.

Tracking Digestion

In the average adult, the digestive canal is about 29 feet long! Think of a 29-foot-long garden hose that winds through your body, helping you break down food into nutrients—the basic materials your body needs.

Do you chew your food thoroughly? Your mouth and teeth are specially designed to chop and chew food. Then the food passes through a tube about ten inches long called the *esophagus*. A series of wave-like muscle contractions automatically moves the food along the digestive tract. This is called *peristalsis*.

Your stomach secretes juices that continue to break down the food particles. Contractions in the stomach push the food into the upper intestine, or *small intestine*. When you get to be an adult, your stomach will hold about 1/2 gallon (2 quarts) of food!

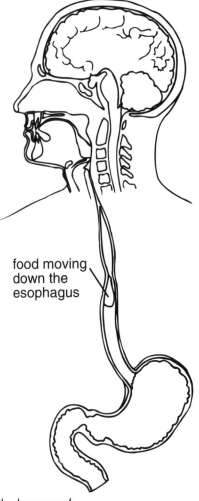

food moving down the esophagus

Directions: Write T for true or F for false before each statement.

_____1. The mouth is not part of the digestive system.

_____2. The teeth are part of the digestive system.

_____3. Food passes from the mouth to the esophagus.

_____4. The esophagus connects the mouth and the stomach.

_____5. The esophagus is about two inches long.

_____6. There are no muscles in the esophagus.

_____7. Food moves automatically through our digestive system.

_____8. Peristalsis is a disease of the digestive system.

_____9. The stomach secretes juices that help break down food.

_____10. Food goes from the stomach to the upper intestine.

Tracking Digestion

Directions: Use the number code to label and color the diagram of the digestive system.

1. The **salivary glands** secrete digestive enzymes to begin the digestive process in the mouth. Color them yellow.
2. The **esophagus** moves the food into the stomach. Color it brown.
3. The **liver** is an important warehouse for the body's nutrients. Color it green.
4. The **stomach** secretes juices that continue to break food particles down. Color it purple.
5. The **gall bladder** stores bile. Color it orange.
6. The **pancreas** secretes juices that help the digestion of food in the small intestine. It also secretes insulin, an important hormone that regulates glucose levels in the blood. Color it pink.
7. In the **small intestine**, body chemicals act with food and nutrients, which are absorbed into the blood. Color the small intestine red.
8. In the **large intestine**, leftover food that is of no use to the body is processed for elimination. Color it blue.

Research: Saliva in your mouth contains enzymes that break down starch and turn it into sugar. Put a piece of dry bread in your mouth and hold it there for a few minutes. Did the bread begin to taste sweet? Try this with two other starchy foods such as potatoes, crackers, corn, or rice. Write a few sentences to tell what happened.

Bonus: A meal stays in your stomach about three hours. It may take three days to pass through your body. Coarse foods that are high in fiber stimulate peristalsis. These high-fiber foods are called *roughage*. Make a list of ten foods that provide roughage for your digestive system.

Chomping And Chewing

When did you get your first baby tooth? You probably got your first tooth between 6 and 9 months. Most children have all of their baby teeth by 2 years of age. Permanent teeth start to come in between the ages of 6 and 12.

Can you count your teeth? By the age of 21, most people have 32 teeth. You may have fewer now because you still have part of your first set of teeth. People get two sets of teeth. The first set is called the *deciduous teeth,* or baby teeth. They appear several months after birth. That set is replaced later by a second set called the *permanent teeth.* A natural cement holds your teeth in place in your gums.

Adults have four different kinds of teeth. Each tooth has a specific job. The *incisor* tooth is shaped like a tiny chisel. It cuts and slices. The *canines (cuspids)* and *premolars (bicuspids)* are pointed. They are designed to grip and tear food. The *molars* are flatter, broader teeth designed to crush and grind. On each side of each jaw, an adult with a complete set of permanent teeth has two incisors, one cuspid, two bicuspids, and three molars.

Directions: Use one word from the text to complete each sentence.

1. A permanent set of teeth has _____ teeth.

2. Adults have_____ different kinds of teeth.

3. Each kind of tooth has a specific_____.

Chomping And Chewing

Directions: Use the number code to color the diagram of the upper and lower permanent teeth.

1. **Upper central incisors**
   Color them green.
2. **Upper lateral incisors**
   Color them blue.
3. **Upper cuspids** (canines)
   Color them purple.
4. **Upper first bicuspids** (premolars)
   Color them orange.
5. **Upper second bicuspids** (premolars)
   Color them red.
6. **Upper first molars**
   Color them gray.
7. **Upper second molars**
   Color them yellow.
8. **Upper third molars** (wisdom teeth)
   Color them brown.
9. **Lower third molars** (wisdom teeth)
   Color them brown.
10. **Lower second molars**
    Color them yellow.
11. **Lower first molars**
    Color them gray.
12. **Lower second bicuspids** (premolars)
    Color them red.
13. **Lower first bicuspids** (premolars)
    Color them orange.
14. **Lower cuspids** (canines)
    Color them purple.
15. **Lower lateral incisors**
    Color them blue.
16. **Lower central incisors**
    Color them green.

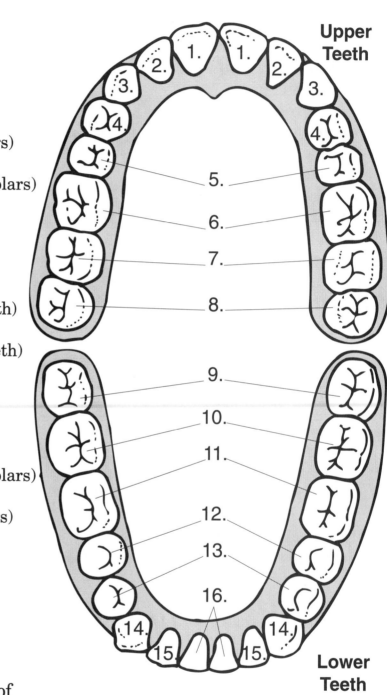

Research: Teeth are made mostly of *calcium phosphate*. Describe calcium phosphate.

Bonus: Use a mirror to study your teeth. Count them. Notice the shape and size of each tooth. Draw a picture of your mouth including each tooth. Label the teeth: central incisors, lateral incisors, cuspids, bicuspids, and molars. Do you have third molars yet?

The Hardest Substance

Do you know what causes cavities? Bacteria do not eat holes in your teeth, but they do feed on food particles in your mouth. When bacteria eat sugar, they make an acid that dissolves the hard minerals in your teeth.

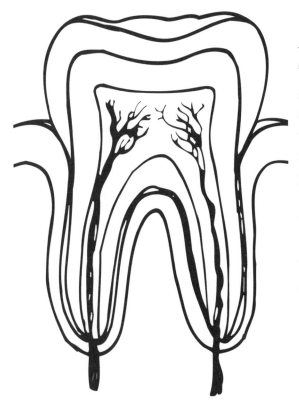

The part of your tooth that you can see when you look in your mouth is the *crown*. The part that is under the gums is called the *root*. Teeth are covered with *enamel,* the hardest substance in the human body. Underneath the enamel, there is a substance called *dentine.* This is slightly softer. It absorbs the impact of chewing. Inside the dentine, there is a pulp chamber. This chamber contains blood vessels that nourish the tooth and nerves.

The canal that extends down the root of the tooth and into the gums is called the *root canal.* Nerves and blood vessels are located in the root canal. These nerves tell us when there is disease or decay in the tooth. Enamel is the hardest substance in the body, yet it can be dissolved by the acid-producing action of bacteria in the mouth.

Directions: Use words from the text to complete the sentences.

1. The top part of the tooth that you can see is called the_____.

2. The bottom part of the tooth that you cannot see is called the _____.

3. The hardest part of a tooth is called the_____.

4. Beneath the enamel of the tooth is the _____.

5. The part of the tooth that absorbs the impact of chewing is_____.

6. At the center of the tooth is the_____.

The Hardest Substance

Directions: Using the information you learned in the text, label the diagram of a tooth. Use the word bank to help you.

Word Bank

enamel   root canal
dentine   nerves and blood vessels
crown   root
pulp chamber

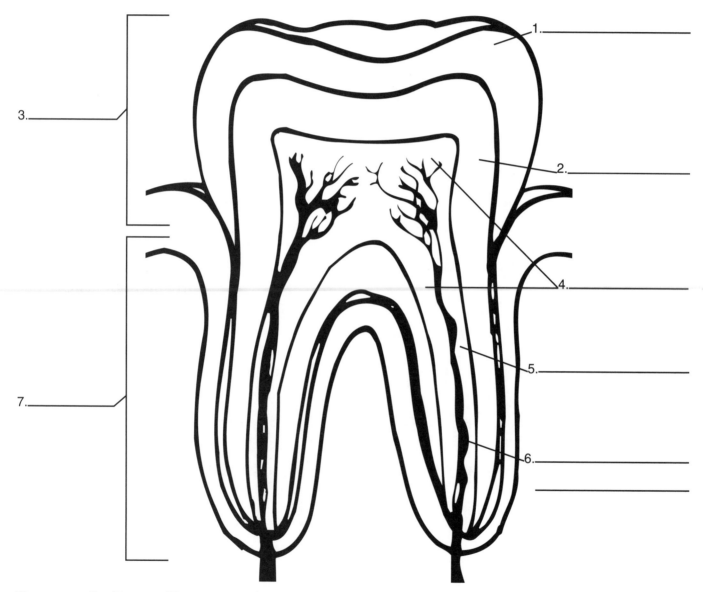

3._____

7._____

1._____

2._____

4._____

5._____

6._____

Research: Draw diagrams showing the names of a set of deciduous (baby) teeth and a set of permanent (adult) teeth.

Bonus: If you get a cavity, the dentine and enamel are permanently damaged. The tooth cannot repair itself. Make a model of a tooth with a cavity. Tell what caused the cavity.

Ten Thousand Taste Buds

You have about 10,000 taste buds on your tongue, but your grandparents probably have fewer. By the age of 60, only about 65% of your taste buds remain. So you can taste less as you grow old.

Taste buds on your tongue distinguish between sweet, sour, bitter, and salty. At the tip of your tongue are the taste buds for sensing sweet things. A little bit farther back on each side of your tongue are most of the taste buds that can taste salty foods. Farther back, at the sides of the tongue and on the roof of your mouth, are the taste buds for sensing sour foods. Right at the very back of your tongue and mouth are bitter-tasting taste buds. Your taste buds work better at warmer temperatures because hot foods release more aromas and flavors.

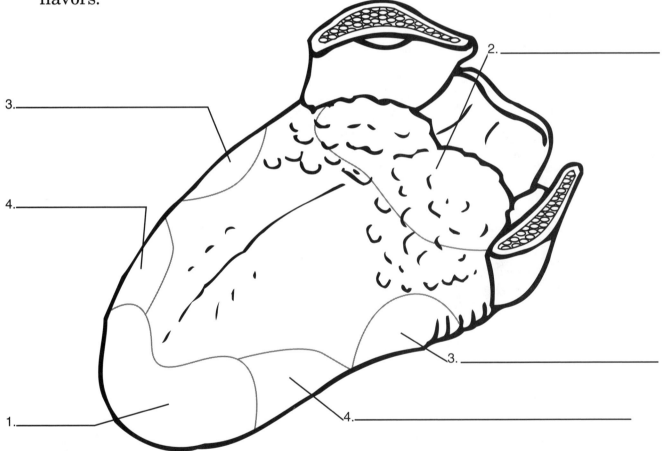

Directions: Use the number code to label and color the taste buds on the diagram of the tongue.

1. Color the **sweet** taste buds pink.
2. Color the **bitter** taste buds blue.
3. Color the **sour** taste buds green.
4. Color the **salty** taste buds red.

Ten Thousand Taste Buds

Directions: Use the number code to label and color the diagram of the mouth, nose, and throat.

1. Color the **nerves of the olfactory bulb** red.
2. Color the **upper lip** light pink.
3. Color the **teeth** white.
4. Color the **mandible** (lower jaw) brown.
5. Color the **nasal passage** yellow.

6. Color the **tongue** dark pink.
7. Color the **epiglottis** green.
8. Color the **esophagus** yellow.
9. Color the **windpipe** (trachea) purple.

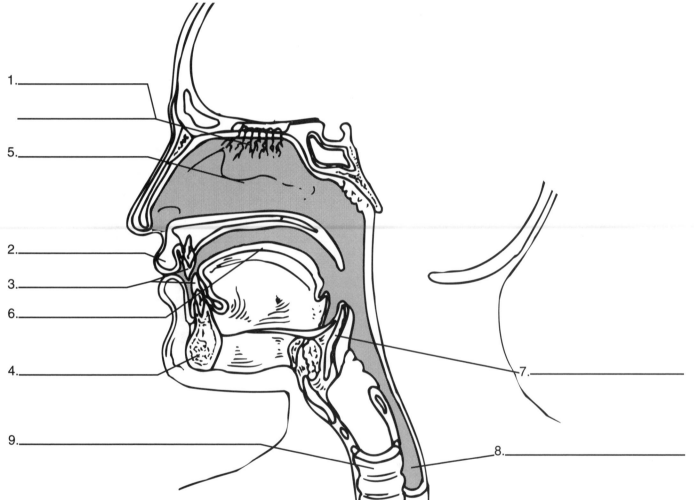

Research: Using information in the text, draw a picture of your tongue. Draw circles where you think the taste buds are for the different areas of taste. Color each area a different color. Label each area sweet, sour, bitter, or salty.

Bonus: Does food taste the same to everyone? Some people like salty or spicy foods and others do not. With a partner make a list of foods that taste "good" and a list of foods that taste "bad."

The Body's Chemical Factory

During your lifetime, you may consume from 60,000 to 100,000 pounds of food! Without enzymes, the body couldn't digest any of that food.

Do you know what your body's largest internal organ is? It's your *liver*. Your liver weighs about 4 1/2 pounds. Your liver also has more separate functions than any of your body's other organs. So far, scientists know of 500 different functions of the liver, and there may be many others yet to be discovered.

This important organ acts like a warehouse for your body's nutrients. It stores or releases sugars, starches, fats, vitamins, and minerals according to your body's needs. It also removes harmful substances from your blood. Your liver filters old blood cells and processes most of the nutrients that are absorbed from the small intestine. Your liver is the most complex organ in the digestive system.

Directions: Circle the letter that is the correct answer for each question.

1. The body's largest internal organ is

   (a) the stomach   (b) the liver   (c) the gall bladder

2. About how much does the liver weigh?

   (a) 4 1/2 ounces   (b) 14 ounces   (c) 4 1/2 pounds

3. The liver acts like a

   (a) warehouse   (b) pump   (c) both a and b

The Body's Chemical Factory

Directions: Use words from the text to fill in the blanks.

1. Name five nutrients that the liver stores.

   _____

   _____

2. Weighing about 4 1/2 pounds, the liver is the _____ internal organ.

3. Which word in the text means "a series of changes by which something develops"? _____

4. The liver detoxifies the _____.

5. The liver filters out old blood _____.

6. The liver processes most of the nutrients that are absorbed from the _____.

7. The liver is the digestive system's most _____ organ.

8. Without enzymes, your body couldn't _____ food.

Research: One of the liver's jobs is to deal with poisonous chemicals in the blood such as drugs and alcohol. Find out what happens to the liver after constant alcohol or drug abuse. Draw a cartoon or make a poster that tells why alcohol is bad for your liver.

Bonus: The liver acts as a filter for the body. To simulate what the liver does for our bodies, use a strainer or a few coffee filters to do this experiment. Pour different substances through the strainer or filters. Try freshly squeezed fruit juice. What happens? What slips through the filter, and what stays in? Write a few sentences about what straining or filtering does to a substance.

Sugar Regulator

Some people with diabetes need insulin shots every day.

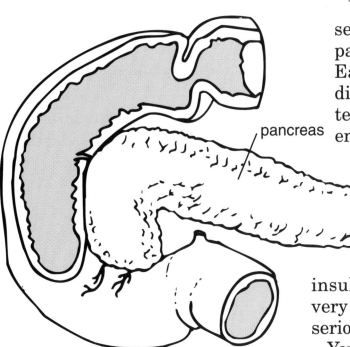

pancreas

Your pancreas is a gland with two separate jobs in digestion. First, the pancreas is like a giant *salivary gland*. Each day it pours one to two pints of digestive juices into the digestive system. The pancreas also manufactures enzymes that digest fats, carbohydrates, and proteins.

Your pancreas also produces *insulin,* a hormone used throughout the body to control your sugar level. Some people don't produce enough insulin, and their blood sugar rises to a very high level after a meal. This can cause serious health problems such as diabetes.

Your pancreas also secretes *glucagon,* a hormone that moves sugar from the liver into the blood when levels are low. Because the level of sugar in your blood is important to your health, your pancreas is a vital gland.

Directions: Use a word or phrase from the text to complete each sentence.

1. The pancreas has_____ jobs in the digestive system.

2. The pancreas manufactures _____ that digest nutrients.

3. Three nutrients that the pancreatic enzymes help digest are

_____.

Sugar Regulator

Directions: Use the text or a dictionary to find the definition of each word. Draw a line to connect each word to its definition.

1. pancreas

2. organs

3. enzyme

4. insulin

5. diabetes

6. hormone

7. disease

a. a sickness in which the body produces little or no insulin

b. a substance produced in plant and animal cells that causes a chemical change

c. a large gland behind the stomach that sends a juice into the small intestine to help digestion

d. a condition of not being healthy

e. The liver and kidneys are examples of these.

f. a hormone of the pancreas that helps the body use sugar and starches

g. a substance formed in an organ and carried in the blood to other parts of the body

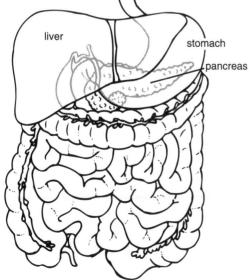

Research: What are *glucose* and *glycogen?* In a few sentences, describe the difference between glucose and glycogen.

Bonus: Do you know a person who has diabetes? Interview the person and ask him these questions. Be sure to record his answers. What is the most difficult thing about having diabetes? What is your biggest worry about the disease? How do you treat the disease?

The Interesting Intestines

**The amount of bacteria that lives within your body could fill a soup can.
All but about a thimbleful live in your intestines.**

Your intestines are part of your digestive tract. Food is kneaded in the stomach and mixed with digestive enzymes. Most digestion occurs in the small intestine. The small intestine is also called the upper intestine and is about 21 feet long.

Most nutrients are absorbed into the blood and the lymph fluid through the intestinal wall. Leftover food that is of no use to the body then passes to the lower, or large, intestine, where it is processed for elimination. The large intestine is about five feet long. The lunch you eat today may take between 15 to 24 hours to pass through your body.

Directions: Write T for true or F for false before each statement.

_____1. After food goes through the stomach, it goes straight to the lower intestine.

_____2. Food is kneaded in the stomach.

_____3. Nutrients are absorbed into the lymph fluid and the blood.

_____4. The large intestine is longer than the upper intestine.

_____5. Most nutrients are absorbed into the blood through the stomach.

_____6. The small intestine is only about five feet long.

_____7. The large intestine is about 21 feet long.

_____8. Sometimes it takes as long as 20 to 30 minutes for food to pass through the digestive system.

The Interesting Intestines

Directions: Use the number code to label and color the diagram of the digestive tract.

1. Color the **esophagus** orange.
2. Color the **liver** blue.
3. Color the **stomach** yellow.
4. Color the **small intestine** (the area where the food goes after it leaves the stomach) red.
5. Color the **large intestine** (the area where the food goes after it leaves the small intestine) purple.

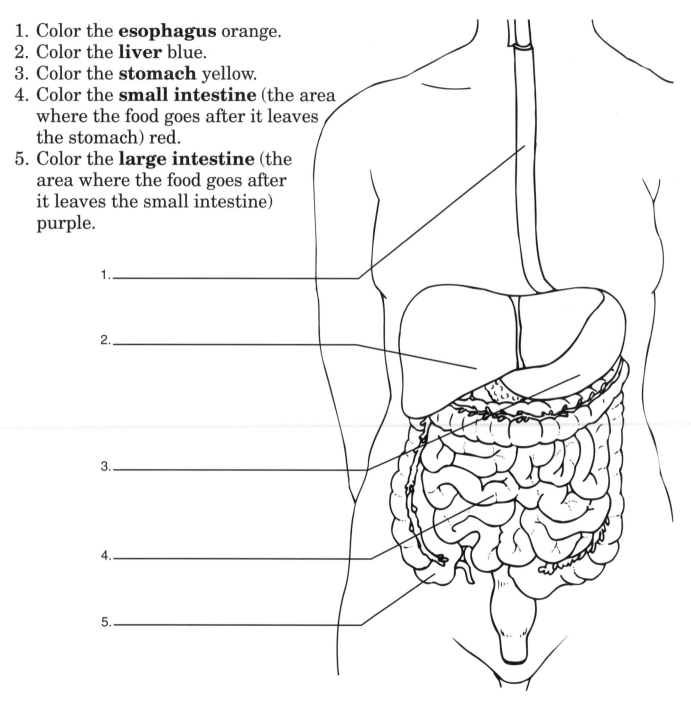

1._____

2._____

3._____

4._____

5._____

Research: Make a list of all the body parts that are involved in the digestive process. You know the approximate lengths of two of those parts. Research the approximate measurements of all the digestive system parts. Add them up to find out how far the food you eat travels within your body.

Bonus: Make a list of six vitamins. List how each vitamin helps your body.

The Body's Messengers

One kind of hormone disorder might cause a person to be as short as two feet or as tall as eight feet.

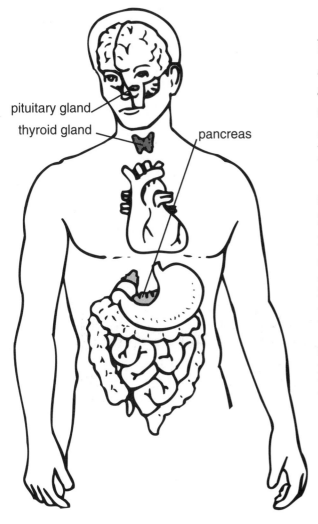

pituitary gland

thyroid gland

pancreas

Your body has a lot of chemicals. The body's most unique chemicals are called *hormones*. They are part of the *endocrine system*. The body has more than 100 different hormones. To be healthy, the body needs a balance between all of the different hormones.

The pancreas secretes insulin when the sugar level rises in the blood, like after a meal. Insulin regulates blood sugar by helping move sugar from the blood into the cells. Adrenaline adjusts your body when you are stressed or frightened, so that you have the necessary blood flow to deal with the situation. Pituitary hormones cause growth changes in the body. Growth hormones make bones grow bigger, and sex hormones make bodies mature into adults.

Directions: Unscramble the words to complete each sentence.

1. The body's most unique chemicals are called (m h n s o e r o)_____.

2. (n s l i i n u)_____ is the hormone that regulates blood sugar.

3. The hormone that helps you when you are stressed is
   (n i a l e a n d r e)_____ .

The Body's Messengers

Directions: Use the text or a dictionary to find the definition of each word. Draw lines to connect the matching terms and definitions.

1. growth hormones

2. insulin

3. sex hormones

4. adrenaline

a. prepares the body for action

b. make your bones grow

c. allows cells to take sugar from your blood to use for fuel

d. change a girl into a woman and a boy into a man

Research: What are *pheromones?* In a short paragraph, describe the difference between pheromones and hormones.

Bonus: On the left side of a sheet of paper, make a list of six terms you have learned while studying the human body. Scramble the definitions on the right side of the page like the exercise above. Give your puzzle to a friend to solve.

Reproduction And Fertilization

All cells contain 46 chromosomes, except the sperm and ovum. Each of these cells has only 23 chromosomes.

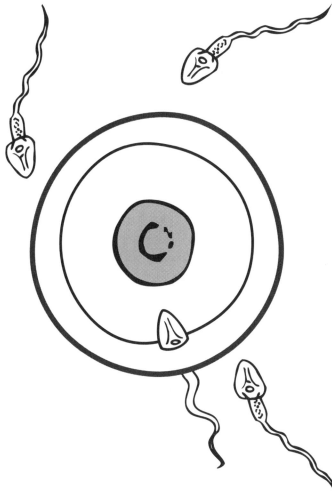

Reproduction is the way people, animals, and plants create more of their own kind. People, most animals, and some plants reproduce when two sex cells are joined. The male sex cell is called a *sperm*. A man makes about 100 million sperm cells every day. The female cell is called an *egg (ovum)*. Females usually make only one egg each month. If not fertilized, the egg will die within a few days.

Male reproductive organs are mostly outside the body. All the female reproductive organs are inside the body. When the sperm and egg come together, they form a *zygote*. After the sperm and ovum join and form a single fertilized egg cell, it has 46 chromosomes.

Directions: Use words from the text to complete the sentences.

1. A female sex cell is called an _____ .

2. When a sperm meets an egg, they form a_____ .

3. A single, fertilized cell has _____ chromosomes.

Reproduction And Fertilization

Directions: Draw lines to connect the matching terms and definitions.

1. Releases one egg per month

2. Releases sperm to fertilize the egg

3. The way people, animals, and plants re-create species

4. The male sex cell is called a

5. The female sex cell is called an

6. When sperm and egg meet, they form a

7. Are mostly outside the body

8. Are all inside the body

9. Egg/ovum

10. Occurs when sperm gets to the egg/ovum

a. sperm

b. reproduction

c. female

d. fertilization

e. female reproductive organs

f. male

g. egg (ovum)

h. is released once a month

i. zygote

j. male reproductive organs

Research: Find out what is different about the fertilization process that creates twins. What are *fraternal twins?*

Bonus: If a woman is fertile for 40 years, about how many eggs does she develop? Look in a book of world records to find the record number of children born to one mother.

Chromosomes And Genes

Chromosomes contain all the necessary information for the cell to develop.

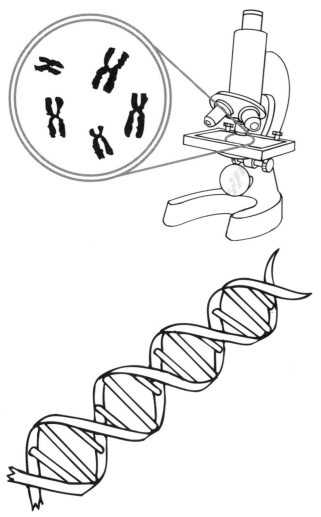

Chromosomes are microscopic, thread-like structures found in the center of every cell. A *gene* is a short section of a chromosome. Each of your genes carries a set of instructions that determines one of your characteristics, such as the color of your hair or eyes. Scientists don't know exactly how many genes we have, but they think each person has at least 100,000 types of genes.

Each male sperm cell and female egg cell contains only 23 chromosomes—half the number found in all other cells. When these two cells come together to make a fertilized egg, the chromosomes mix to make 46 chromosomes. That means that the baby will grow up with a mixture of features from both of its parents.

DNA is the complicated chemical substance that makes up your genes and chromosomes. DNA contains the genetic information that is passed from one generation to the next.

Directions: Use numbers from the text to answer the questions.

1. Most cells have _____ chromosomes.

2. Sex cells have _____ chromosomes.

3. Scientists think we have at least _____ types of genes.

4. A fertilized egg has_____ chromosomes.

Chromosomes And Genes

Directions: Read each question below. Circle *mother* or *father,* depending on which one you think you inherited that trait from. If both your parents have red hair and you have red hair, circle *mother* and *father*. If you don't have red hair and both your parents have red hair, don't circle either one.

1. Are you left-handed or right-handed? .... mother .... father

2. Color of your hair? .... mother .... father

3. Is your hair straight or curly? .... mother .... father

4. Do you have a widow's peak? .... mother .... father

5. Color of your eyes? .... mother .... father

6. Long or short eyelashes? .... mother .... father

7. Curly or straight eyelashes? .... mother .... father

8. Shape of eyebrows? .... mother .... father

9. Do you have dimples? .... mother .... father

10. Is your nose turned up? .... mother .... father

11. Are your earlobes free or connected? .... mother .... father

12. Are your earlobes pointed or rounded? .... mother .... father

13. Do you have freckles? .... mother .... father

14. Can you fold your tongue in a roll? .... mother .... father

Research: Find out what *asexual* means. Write a sentence about it.

Bonus: Talk to a parent and make a list of traits you have in common with your grandparents and great-grandparents.

The Fascinating Facts About The Human Body Game

Getting Ready To Play

1. On heavy paper or light cardboard, reproduce the game cards on pages 104–118. You may choose to color-code the cards by reproducing the true/false questions on one color of paper, the multiple-choice questions on a second color, and the fill-in-the-blank questions on a third color. If the cards will be used many times, laminate them.
2. Choose two to four teams with two to four players per team. Each team may want to pick a team name and wear matching T-shirts and caps.
3. Sort the cards into three stacks and shuffle each stack.
4. Explain the point system to the students:
    true/false = 5 points
    multiple choice = 10 points
    fill in the blank = 15 points

How To Play

1. One member of the first team chooses which type of question he wants to receive—true/false, multiple choice, or fill in the blank.
2. The teacher reads an appropriate question from the top of the deck. If that player answers correctly, his team receives the appropriate number of points.
3. If he answers incorrectly, one player on another team gets the opportunity to answer the question. (If it was a true/false question, the opponent will automatically get it correct if he was listening.) If he answers correctly, his team gets the points. If he answers incorrectly, no one gets the points and the teacher gives the correct answer.
4. Then one player from the next team gets to choose the type of question he wants the opportunity to answer.
5. The game continues until one team reaches 50 points. To extend the game, play until one team reaches 100 points.

Variation

Use as flash cards with the whole class. Shuffle all of the cards into one stack and ask questions from the top of the deck. Give one point for each correct answer.

Game Cards

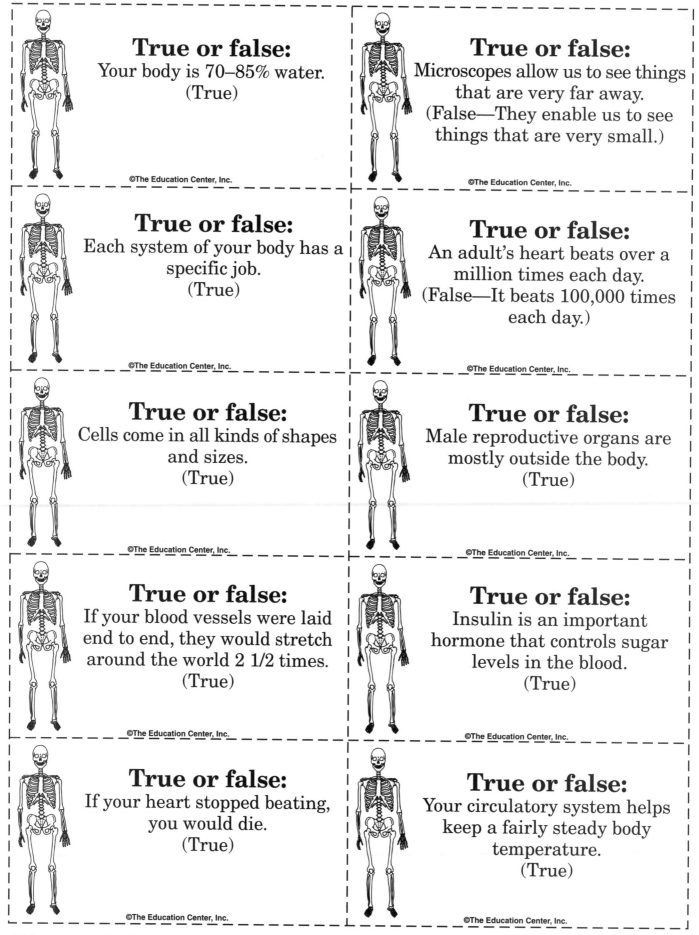

True or false:
Your body is 70–85% water.
(True)

©The Education Center, Inc.

True or false:
Microscopes allow us to see things that are very far away.
(False—They enable us to see things that are very small.)

©The Education Center, Inc.

True or false:
Each system of your body has a specific job.
(True)

©The Education Center, Inc.

True or false:
An adult's heart beats over a million times each day.
(False—It beats 100,000 times each day.)

©The Education Center, Inc.

True or false:
Cells come in all kinds of shapes and sizes.
(True)

©The Education Center, Inc.

True or false:
Male reproductive organs are mostly outside the body.
(True)

©The Education Center, Inc.

True or false:
If your blood vessels were laid end to end, they would stretch around the world 2 1/2 times.
(True)

©The Education Center, Inc.

True or false:
Insulin is an important hormone that controls sugar levels in the blood.
(True)

©The Education Center, Inc.

True or false:
If your heart stopped beating, you would die.
(True)

©The Education Center, Inc.

True or false:
Your circulatory system helps keep a fairly steady body temperature.
(True)

©The Education Center, Inc.

Fascinating Facts About The Human Body—Grades 4–6 • ©1995 The Education Center, Inc. • TEC370

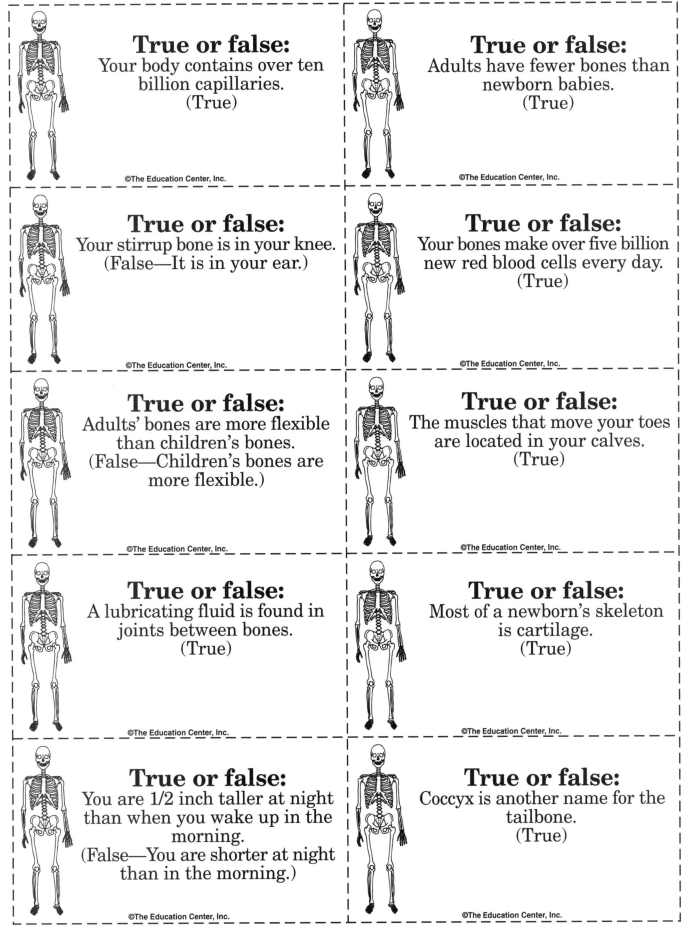

True or false:
Your body contains over ten
billion capillaries.
(True)

©The Education Center, Inc.

True or false:
Adults have fewer bones than
newborn babies.
(True)

©The Education Center, Inc.

True or false:
Your stirrup bone is in your knee.
(False—It is in your ear.)

©The Education Center, Inc.

True or false:
Your bones make over five billion
new red blood cells every day.
(True)

©The Education Center, Inc.

True or false:
Adults' bones are more flexible
than children's bones.
(False—Children's bones are
more flexible.)

©The Education Center, Inc.

True or false:
The muscles that move your toes
are located in your calves.
(True)

©The Education Center, Inc.

True or false:
A lubricating fluid is found in
joints between bones.
(True)

©The Education Center, Inc.

True or false:
Most of a newborn's skeleton
is cartilage.
(True)

©The Education Center, Inc.

True or false:
You are 1/2 inch taller at night
than when you wake up in the
morning.
(False—You are shorter at night
than in the morning.)

©The Education Center, Inc.

True or false:
Coccyx is another name for the
tailbone.
(True)

©The Education Center, Inc.

Game Cards

True or false:
Nerves can pass messages along at nearly 250 miles per hour.
(True)

©The Education Center, Inc.

True or false:
Your brain is always working; it never stops.
(True)

©The Education Center, Inc.

True or false:
Your brain is made up of about 100 billion nerve cells.
(True)

©The Education Center, Inc.

True or false:
The male sex cell is called ovum.
(False—The male sex cell is called sperm.)

©The Education Center, Inc.

True or false:
If you touch a hot stove, the nerves in your fingers will send a message to the nerves in your spinal cord.
(True)

©The Education Center, Inc.

True or false:
Cushioning is what cartilage does for your bones.
(True)

©The Education Center, Inc.

True or false:
Every second, millions of cells in your body die and are replaced by new ones.
(True)

©The Education Center, Inc.

True or false:
Your shoulder is the most mobile joint in your body.
(True)

©The Education Center, Inc.

True or false:
Normally, food takes three to five hours to pass through the body.
(False—It may take up to 3 days)

©The Education Center, Inc.

True or false:
An adult's stomach can hold about six gallons of food.
(False—It can hold about 1/2 gallon of food.)

©The Education Center, Inc.

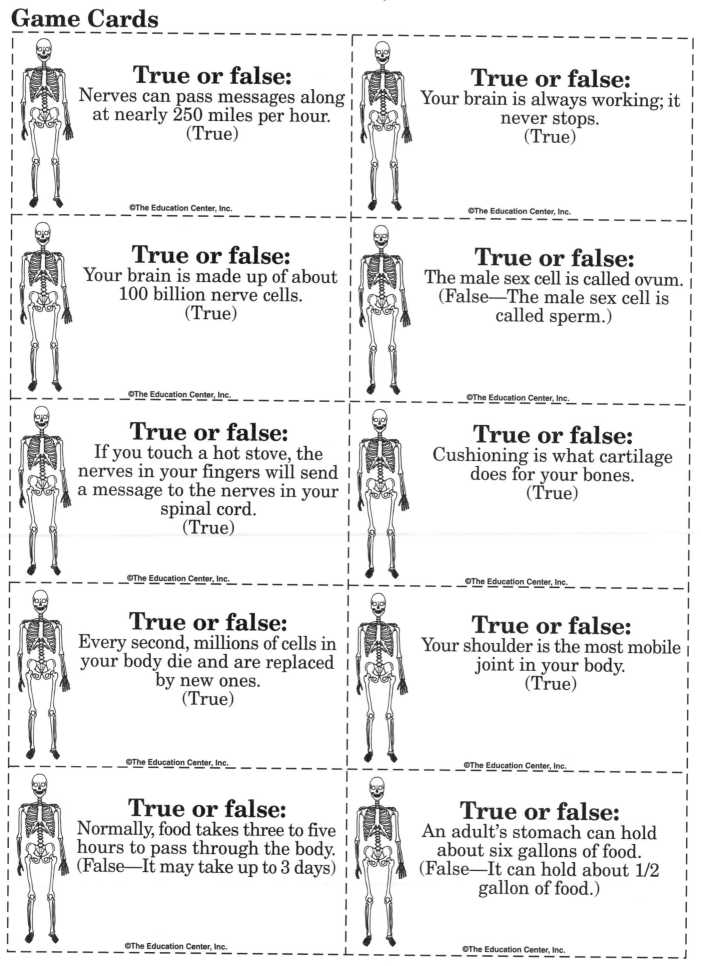

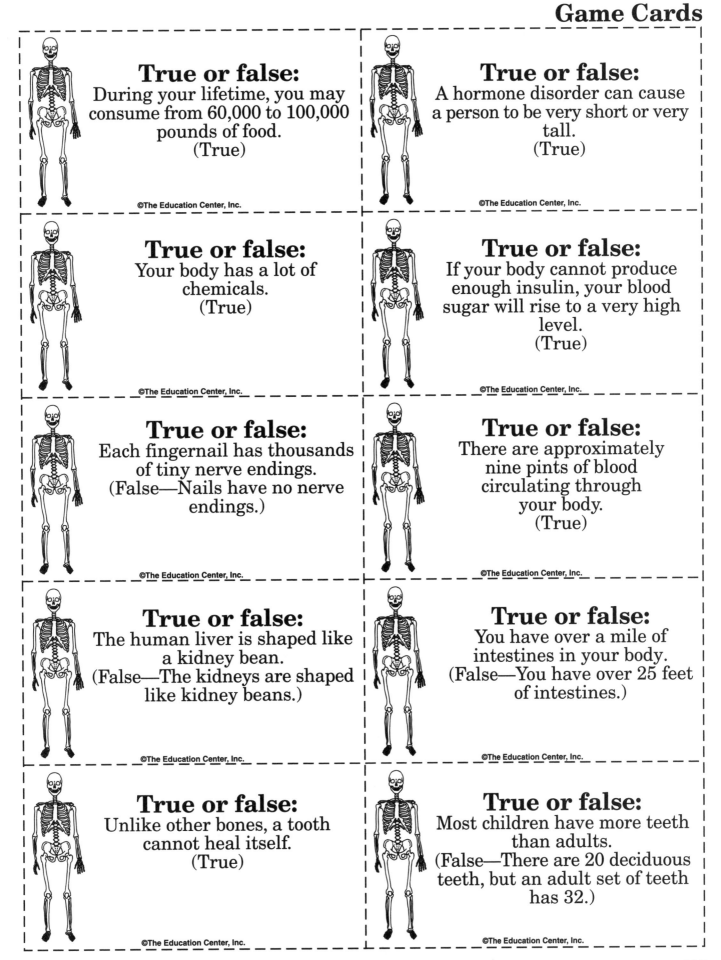

True or false:
During your lifetime, you may consume from 60,000 to 100,000 pounds of food.
(True)

©The Education Center, Inc.

True or false:
A hormone disorder can cause a person to be very short or very tall.
(True)

©The Education Center, Inc.

True or false:
Your body has a lot of chemicals.
(True)

©The Education Center, Inc.

True or false:
If your body cannot produce enough insulin, your blood sugar will rise to a very high level.
(True)

©The Education Center, Inc.

True or false:
Each fingernail has thousands of tiny nerve endings.
(False—Nails have no nerve endings.)

©The Education Center, Inc.

True or false:
There are approximately nine pints of blood circulating through your body.
(True)

©The Education Center, Inc.

True or false:
The human liver is shaped like a kidney bean.
(False—The kidneys are shaped like kidney beans.)

©The Education Center, Inc.

True or false:
You have over a mile of intestines in your body.
(False—You have over 25 feet of intestines.)

©The Education Center, Inc.

True or false:
Unlike other bones, a tooth cannot heal itself.
(True)

©The Education Center, Inc.

True or false:
Most children have more teeth than adults.
(False—There are 20 deciduous teeth, but an adult set of teeth has 32.)

©The Education Center, Inc.

Game Cards

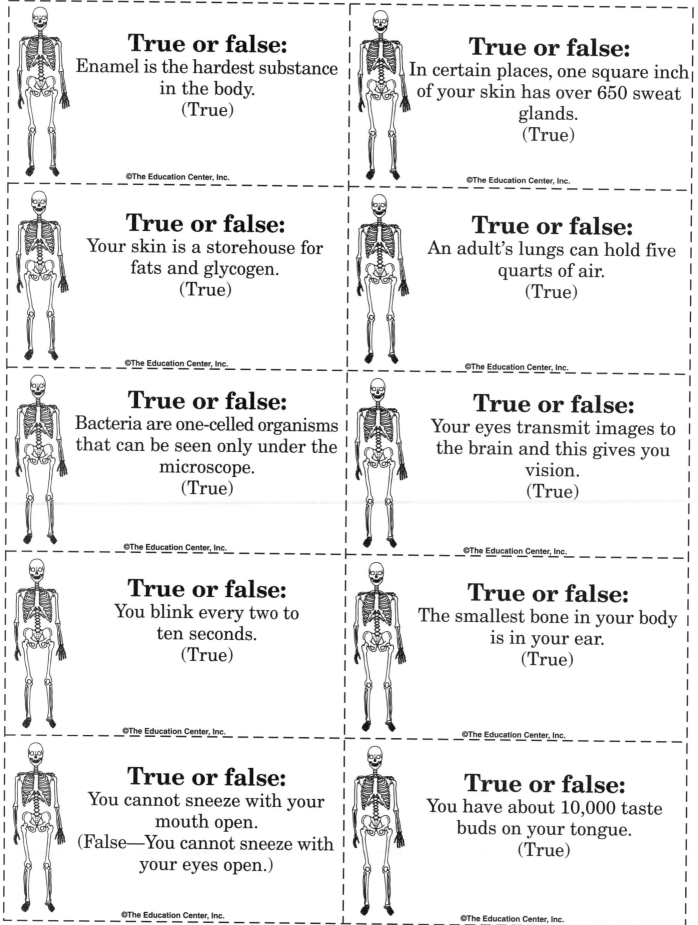

True or false:
Enamel is the hardest substance
in the body.
(True)

True or false:
In certain places, one square inch
of your skin has over 650 sweat
glands.
(True)

True or false:
Your skin is a storehouse for
fats and glycogen.
(True)

True or false:
An adult's lungs can hold five
quarts of air.
(True)

True or false:
Bacteria are one-celled organisms
that can be seen only under the
microscope.
(True)

True or false:
Your eyes transmit images to
the brain and this gives you
vision.
(True)

True or false:
You blink every two to
ten seconds.
(True)

True or false:
The smallest bone in your body
is in your ear.
(True)

True or false:
You cannot sneeze with your
mouth open.
(False—You cannot sneeze with
your eyes open.)

True or false:
You have about 10,000 taste
buds on your tongue.
(True)

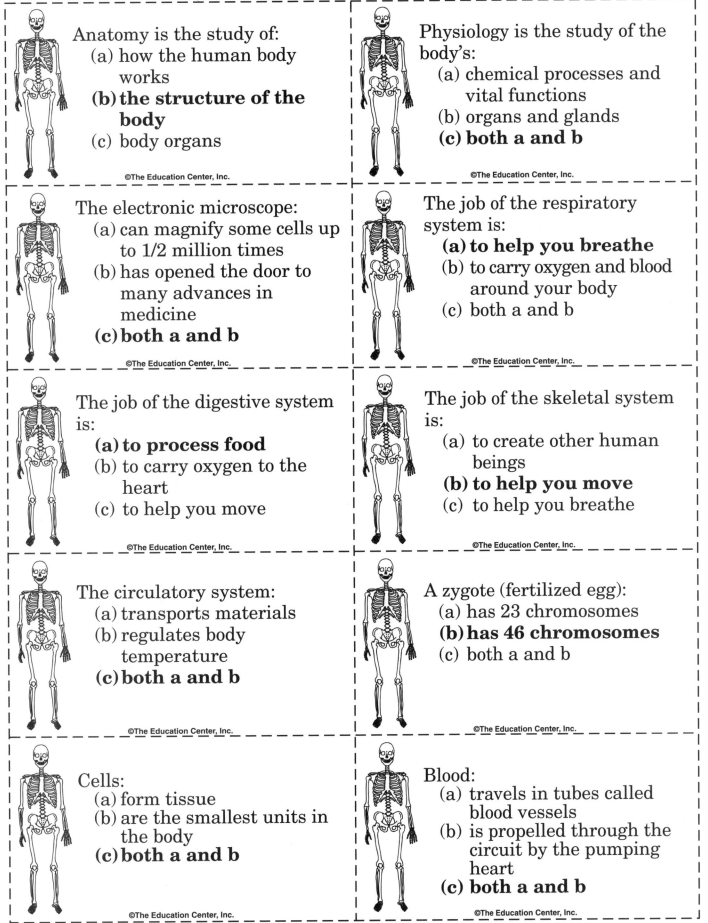

Anatomy is the study of:
(a) how the human body works
(b) the structure of the body
(c) body organs

©The Education Center, Inc.

Physiology is the study of the body's:
(a) chemical processes and vital functions
(b) organs and glands
(c) both a and b

©The Education Center, Inc.

The electronic microscope:
(a) can magnify some cells up to 1/2 million times
(b) has opened the door to many advances in medicine
(c) both a and b

©The Education Center, Inc.

The job of the respiratory system is:
(a) to help you breathe
(b) to carry oxygen and blood around your body
(c) both a and b

©The Education Center, Inc.

The job of the digestive system is:
(a) to process food
(b) to carry oxygen to the heart
(c) to help you move

©The Education Center, Inc.

The job of the skeletal system is:
(a) to create other human beings
(b) to help you move
(c) to help you breathe

©The Education Center, Inc.

The circulatory system:
(a) transports materials
(b) regulates body temperature
(c) both a and b

©The Education Center, Inc.

A zygote (fertilized egg):
(a) has 23 chromosomes
(b) has 46 chromosomes
(c) both a and b

©The Education Center, Inc.

Cells:
(a) form tissue
(b) are the smallest units in the body
(c) both a and b

©The Education Center, Inc.

Blood:
(a) travels in tubes called blood vessels
(b) is propelled through the circuit by the pumping heart
(c) both a and b

©The Education Center, Inc.

Game Cards

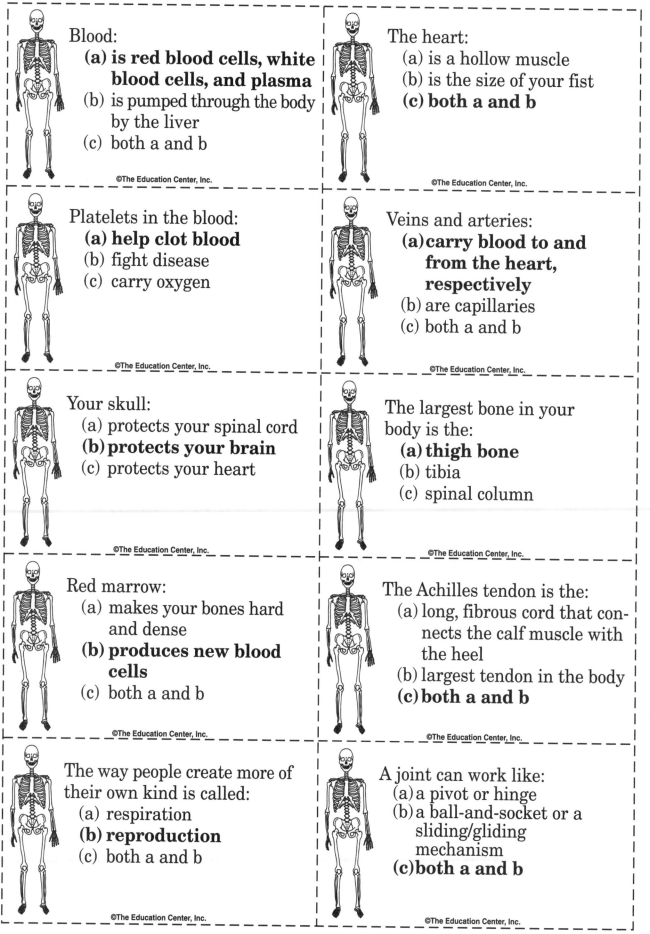

Blood:
- **(a) is red blood cells, white blood cells, and plasma**
- (b) is pumped through the body by the liver
- (c) both a and b

©The Education Center, Inc.

The heart:
- (a) is a hollow muscle
- (b) is the size of your fist
- **(c) both a and b**

©The Education Center, Inc.

Platelets in the blood:
- **(a) help clot blood**
- (b) fight disease
- (c) carry oxygen

©The Education Center, Inc.

Veins and arteries:
- **(a) carry blood to and from the heart, respectively**
- (b) are capillaries
- (c) both a and b

©The Education Center, Inc.

Your skull:
- (a) protects your spinal cord
- **(b) protects your brain**
- (c) protects your heart

©The Education Center, Inc.

The largest bone in your body is the:
- **(a) thigh bone**
- (b) tibia
- (c) spinal column

©The Education Center, Inc.

Red marrow:
- (a) makes your bones hard and dense
- **(b) produces new blood cells**
- (c) both a and b

©The Education Center, Inc.

The Achilles tendon is the:
- (a) long, fibrous cord that connects the calf muscle with the heel
- (b) largest tendon in the body
- **(c) both a and b**

©The Education Center, Inc.

The way people create more of their own kind is called:
- (a) respiration
- **(b) reproduction**
- (c) both a and b

©The Education Center, Inc.

A joint can work like:
- (a) a pivot or hinge
- (b) a ball-and-socket or a sliding/gliding mechanism
- **(c) both a and b**

©The Education Center, Inc.

Fascinating Facts About The Human Body—Grades 4–6 • ©1995 The Education Center, Inc. • TEC370

Cartilage:
(a) lines joints to minimize friction between bones
(b) makes up part of a baby's skeleton
(c) both a and b

©The Education Center, Inc.

The backbone:
(a) has 33 bones stacked on top of each other
(b) gives you mobility and flexibility
(c) both a and b

©The Education Center, Inc.

At the tip of the backbone is the:
(a) sacrum
(b) coccyx
(c) tibia

©The Education Center, Inc.

The spinal cord:
(a) links the brain to the rest of the body
(b) is a bundle of nerves
(c) both a and b

©The Education Center, Inc.

The brain:
(a) is about 2% of your body's weight
(b) consumes 20% of the energy produced by your body
(c) both a and b

©The Education Center, Inc.

The brain:
(a) needs a lot of blood
(b) is built of 100 billion nerve cells
(c) both a and b

©The Education Center, Inc.

Your head:
(a) houses your brain
(b) houses your sensory centers
(c) both a and b

©The Education Center, Inc.

The knee:
(a) is a ball-and-socket joint
(b) is a hinged joint
(c) is a pivot joint

©The Education Center, Inc.

The elbow:
(a) is a ball-and-socket joint
(b) is a hinged joint
(c) is a pivot joint

©The Education Center, Inc.

The shoulder:
(a) is the most mobile joint in the body
(b) can rotate 360 degrees
(c) both a and b

©The Education Center, Inc.

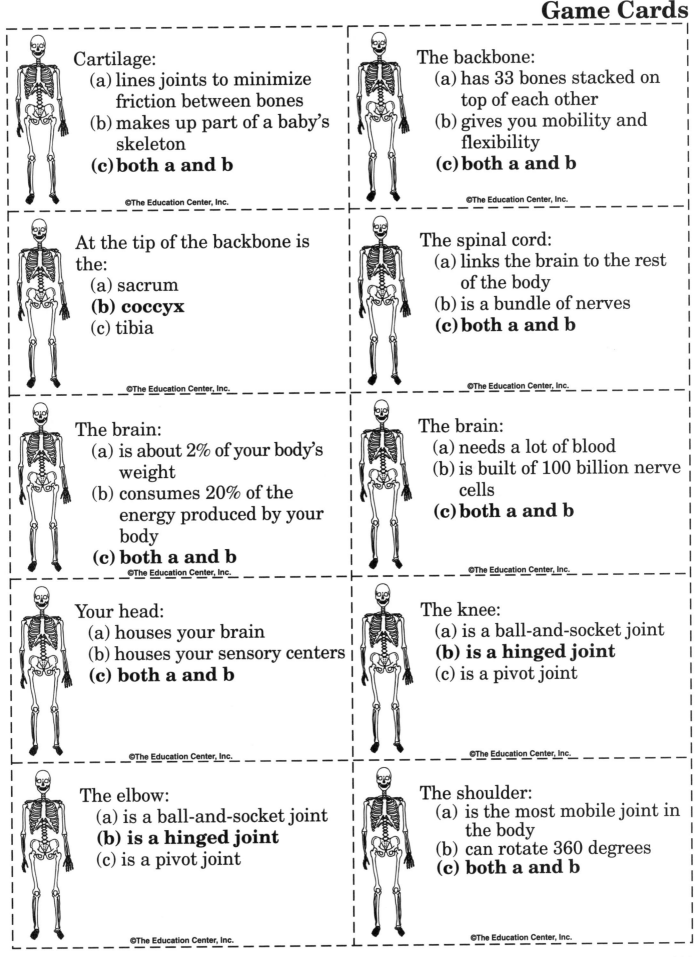

Game Cards

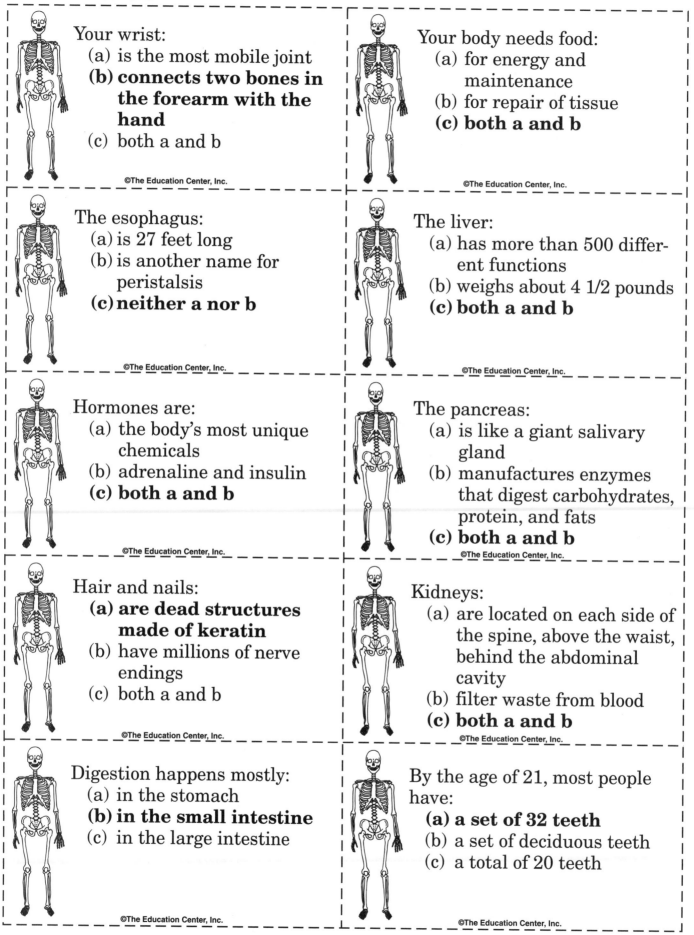

Your wrist:
- (a) is the most mobile joint
- **(b) connects two bones in the forearm with the hand**
- (c) both a and b

©The Education Center, Inc.

Your body needs food:
- (a) for energy and maintenance
- (b) for repair of tissue
- **(c) both a and b**

©The Education Center, Inc.

The esophagus:
- (a) is 27 feet long
- (b) is another name for peristalsis
- **(c) neither a nor b**

©The Education Center, Inc.

The liver:
- (a) has more than 500 different functions
- (b) weighs about 4 1/2 pounds
- **(c) both a and b**

©The Education Center, Inc.

Hormones are:
- (a) the body's most unique chemicals
- (b) adrenaline and insulin
- **(c) both a and b**

©The Education Center, Inc.

The pancreas:
- (a) is like a giant salivary gland
- (b) manufactures enzymes that digest carbohydrates, protein, and fats
- **(c) both a and b**

©The Education Center, Inc.

Hair and nails:
- **(a) are dead structures made of keratin**
- (b) have millions of nerve endings
- (c) both a and b

©The Education Center, Inc.

Kidneys:
- (a) are located on each side of the spine, above the waist, behind the abdominal cavity
- (b) filter waste from blood
- **(c) both a and b**

©The Education Center, Inc.

Digestion happens mostly:
- (a) in the stomach
- **(b) in the small intestine**
- (c) in the large intestine

©The Education Center, Inc.

By the age of 21, most people have:
- **(a) a set of 32 teeth**
- (b) a set of deciduous teeth
- (c) a total of 20 teeth

©The Education Center, Inc.

Fascinating Facts About The Human Body—Grades 4–6 • ©1995 The Education Center, Inc. • TEC370

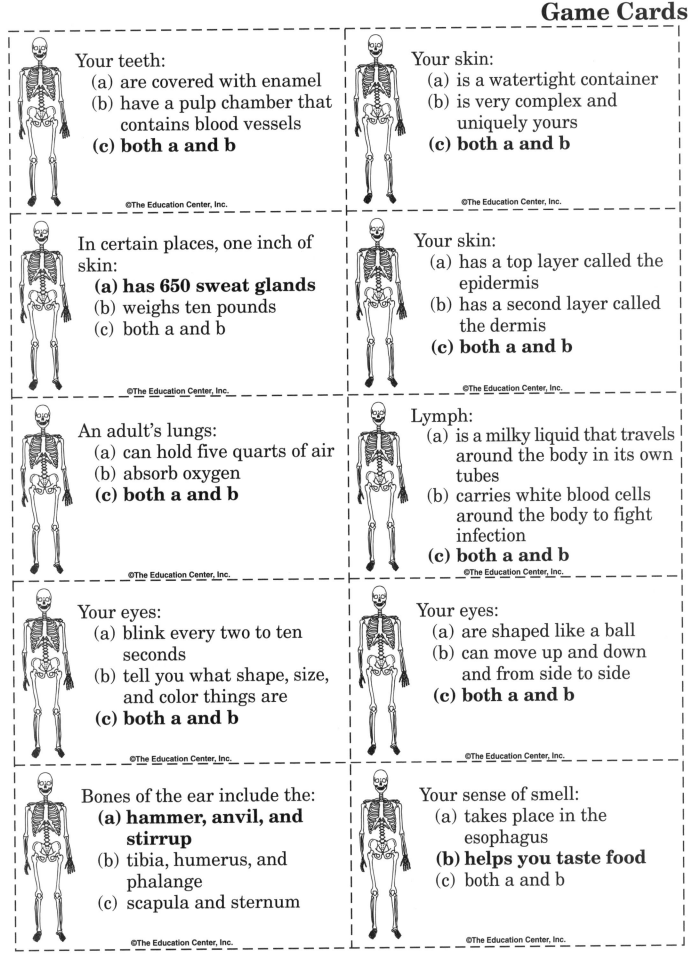

Your teeth:
(a) are covered with enamel
(b) have a pulp chamber that contains blood vessels
(c) both a and b

©The Education Center, Inc.

Your skin:
(a) is a watertight container
(b) is very complex and uniquely yours
(c) both a and b

©The Education Center, Inc.

In certain places, one inch of skin:
(a) has 650 sweat glands
(b) weighs ten pounds
(c) both a and b

©The Education Center, Inc.

Your skin:
(a) has a top layer called the epidermis
(b) has a second layer called the dermis
(c) both a and b

©The Education Center, Inc.

An adult's lungs:
(a) can hold five quarts of air
(b) absorb oxygen
(c) both a and b

©The Education Center, Inc.

Lymph:
(a) is a milky liquid that travels around the body in its own tubes
(b) carries white blood cells around the body to fight infection
(c) both a and b

©The Education Center, Inc.

Your eyes:
(a) blink every two to ten seconds
(b) tell you what shape, size, and color things are
(c) both a and b

©The Education Center, Inc.

Your eyes:
(a) are shaped like a ball
(b) can move up and down and from side to side
(c) both a and b

©The Education Center, Inc.

Bones of the ear include the:
(a) hammer, anvil, and stirrup
(b) tibia, humerus, and phalange
(c) scapula and sternum

©The Education Center, Inc.

Your sense of smell:
(a) takes place in the esophagus
(b) helps you taste food
(c) both a and b

©The Education Center, Inc.

Game Cards

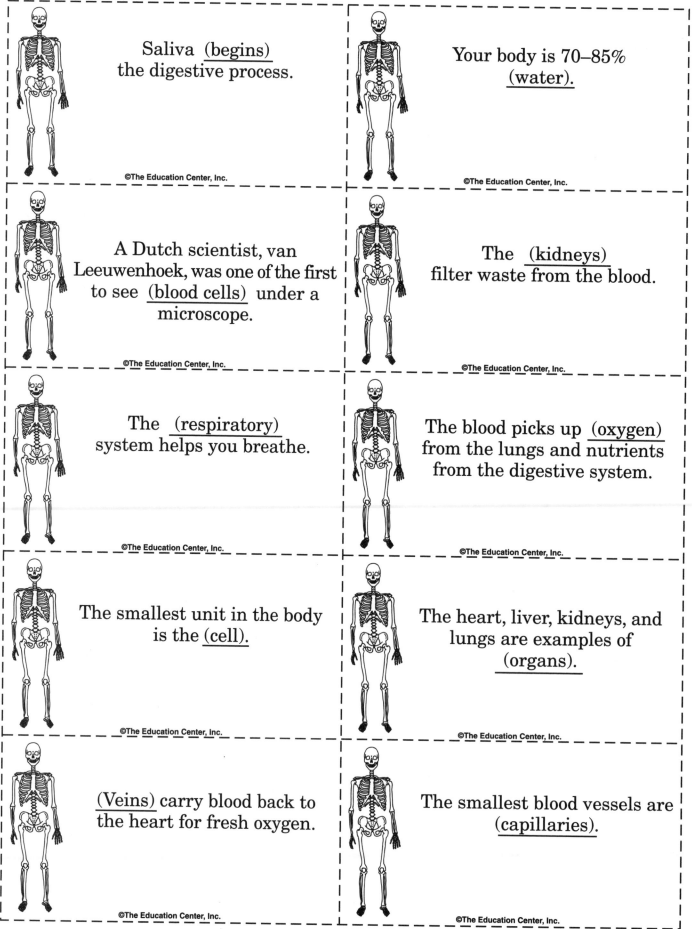

Saliva (begins) the digestive process.

©The Education Center, Inc.

Your body is 70–85% (water).

©The Education Center, Inc.

A Dutch scientist, van Leeuwenhoek, was one of the first to see (blood cells) under a microscope.

©The Education Center, Inc.

The (kidneys) filter waste from the blood.

©The Education Center, Inc.

The (respiratory) system helps you breathe.

©The Education Center, Inc.

The blood picks up (oxygen) from the lungs and nutrients from the digestive system.

©The Education Center, Inc.

The smallest unit in the body is the (cell).

©The Education Center, Inc.

The heart, liver, kidneys, and lungs are examples of (organs).

©The Education Center, Inc.

(Veins) carry blood back to the heart for fresh oxygen.

©The Education Center, Inc.

The smallest blood vessels are (capillaries).

©The Education Center, Inc.

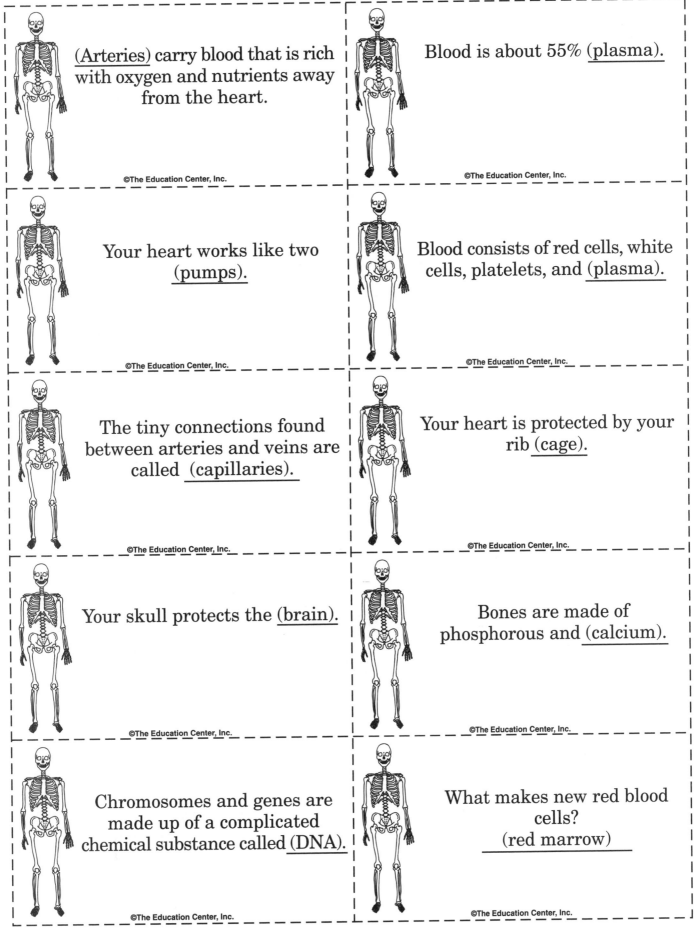

(Arteries) carry blood that is rich with oxygen and nutrients away from the heart.

©The Education Center, Inc.

Blood is about 55% (plasma).

©The Education Center, Inc.

Your heart works like two (pumps).

©The Education Center, Inc.

Blood consists of red cells, white cells, platelets, and (plasma).

©The Education Center, Inc.

The tiny connections found between arteries and veins are called (capillaries).

©The Education Center, Inc.

Your heart is protected by your rib (cage).

©The Education Center, Inc.

Your skull protects the (brain).

©The Education Center, Inc.

Bones are made of phosphorous and (calcium).

©The Education Center, Inc.

Chromosomes and genes are made up of a complicated chemical substance called (DNA).

©The Education Center, Inc.

What makes new red blood cells?
(red marrow)

©The Education Center, Inc.

Game Cards

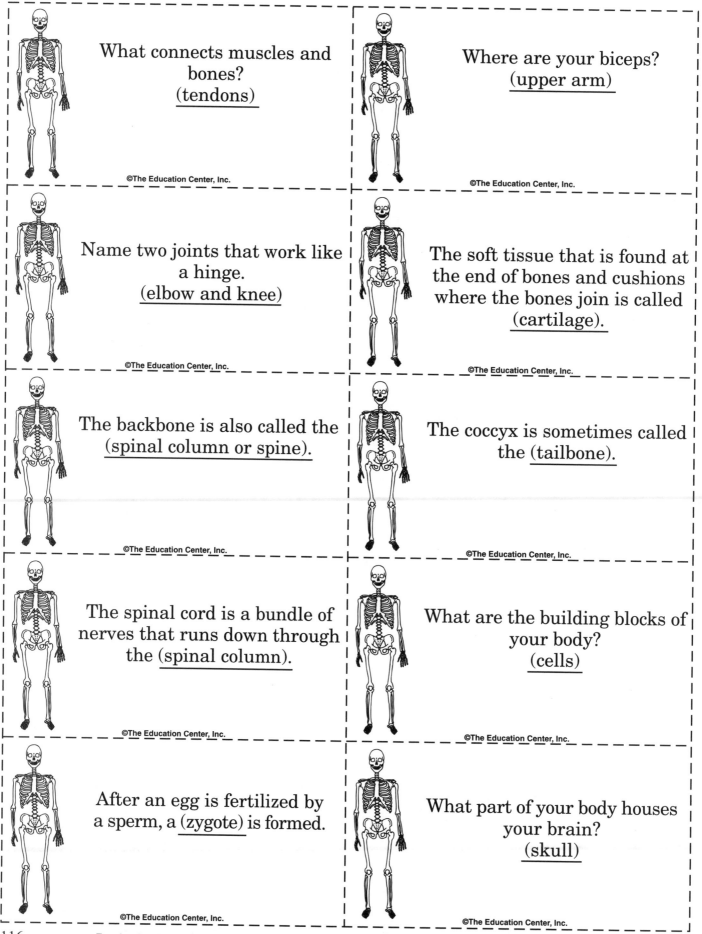

What connects muscles and bones?
(tendons)
©The Education Center, Inc.

Where are your biceps?
(upper arm)
©The Education Center, Inc.

Name two joints that work like a hinge.
(elbow and knee)
©The Education Center, Inc.

The soft tissue that is found at the end of bones and cushions where the bones join is called (cartilage).
©The Education Center, Inc.

The backbone is also called the (spinal column or spine).
©The Education Center, Inc.

The coccyx is sometimes called the (tailbone).
©The Education Center, Inc.

The spinal cord is a bundle of nerves that runs down through the (spinal column).
©The Education Center, Inc.

What are the building blocks of your body?
(cells)
©The Education Center, Inc.

After an egg is fertilized by a sperm, a (zygote) is formed.
©The Education Center, Inc.

What part of your body houses your brain?
(skull)
©The Education Center, Inc.

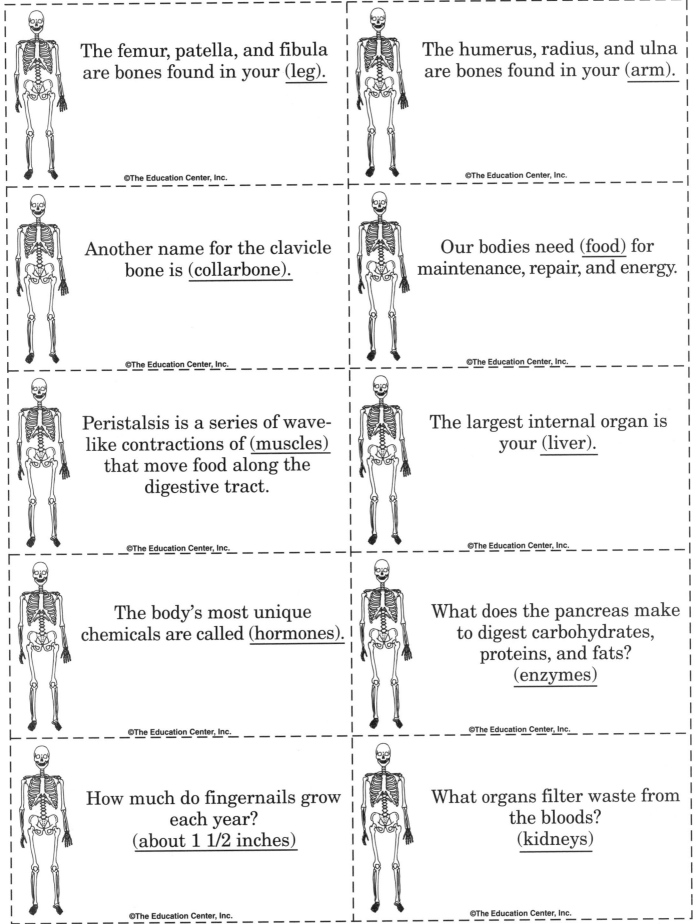

The femur, patella, and fibula are bones found in your (leg).

©The Education Center, Inc.

The humerus, radius, and ulna are bones found in your (arm).

©The Education Center, Inc.

Another name for the clavicle bone is (collarbone).

©The Education Center, Inc.

Our bodies need (food) for maintenance, repair, and energy.

©The Education Center, Inc.

Peristalsis is a series of wave-like contractions of (muscles) that move food along the digestive tract.

©The Education Center, Inc.

The largest internal organ is your (liver).

©The Education Center, Inc.

The body's most unique chemicals are called (hormones).

©The Education Center, Inc.

What does the pancreas make to digest carbohydrates, proteins, and fats? (enzymes)

©The Education Center, Inc.

How much do fingernails grow each year? (about 1 1/2 inches)

©The Education Center, Inc.

What organs filter waste from the bloods? (kidneys)

©The Education Center, Inc.

Game Cards

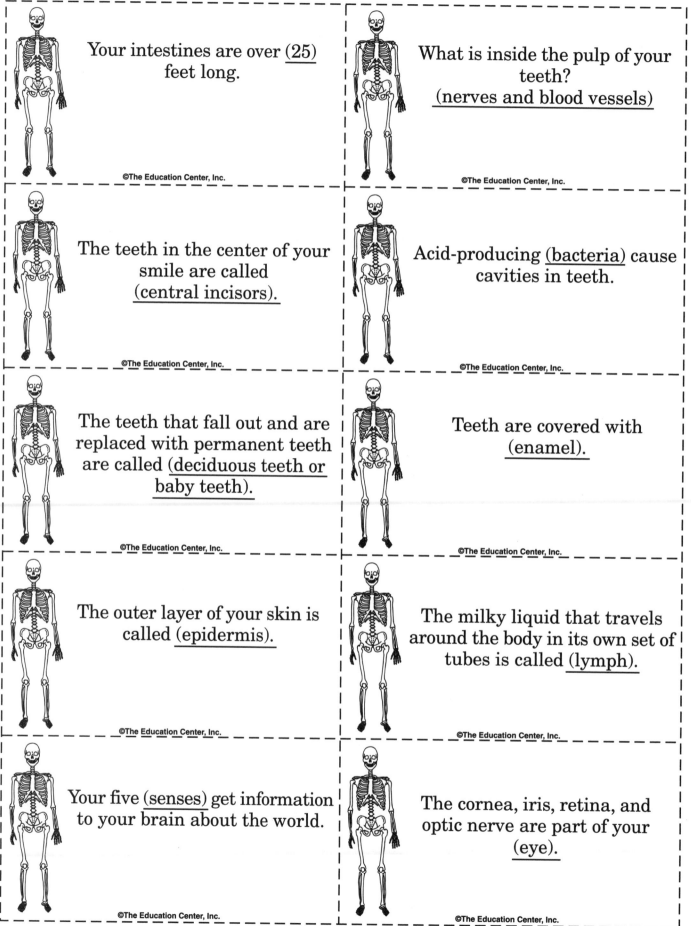

Your intestines are over (25) feet long.

©The Education Center, Inc.

What is inside the pulp of your teeth?
(nerves and blood vessels)

©The Education Center, Inc.

The teeth in the center of your smile are called (central incisors).

©The Education Center, Inc.

Acid-producing (bacteria) cause cavities in teeth.

©The Education Center, Inc.

The teeth that fall out and are replaced with permanent teeth are called (deciduous teeth or baby teeth).

©The Education Center, Inc.

Teeth are covered with (enamel).

©The Education Center, Inc.

The outer layer of your skin is called (epidermis).

©The Education Center, Inc.

The milky liquid that travels around the body in its own set of tubes is called (lymph).

©The Education Center, Inc.

Your five (senses) get information to your brain about the world.

©The Education Center, Inc.

The cornea, iris, retina, and optic nerve are part of your (eye).

©The Education Center, Inc.

Answer Key

Page 5
1. a
2. b
3. a

Page 6
1. c 4. b
2. c 5. b
3. a

Page 8
1. blood cells
2. microscope
3. bacteria
4. science
5. causes

Page 11
1. T 5. F
2. T 6. T
3. F 7. F
4. T 8. T

Page 12
Bonus:
minute = 60,000,000
hour = 3,600,000,000
day = 86,400,000,000
week = 604,800,000,000

Page 13
1. b 3. c
2. c 4. b

Page 14
1. Cells form body tissue.
2. The heart, liver, kidneys, and lungs are organs.
3. Organs work together as a system.
4. (Answers will vary.) Cells are the building blocks and the workhorses of your body. Cells are about 1/1,000 of an inch across. Cells do tremendous jobs.
5. Some cells fight disease, some transport oxygen, and some produce movement. Some cells manufacture proteins, chemicals, or liquids. (See the text for more answers.)

6. There are approximately 200 different kinds of cells in your body.

Page 15
1. circulatory
2. heart, blood vessels, and blood
3. transports materials and regulates body temperature

Page 16
1. blood vessels
2. lungs
3. nutrients
4. to the cells
5. it is brought to the surface by blood vessels

Page 17
1. T 4. F
2. T 5. F
3. F

Page 19
1. 55% 4. 43%
2. 2% 5. 10%
3. 90%

Page 20
43% = red
2% = white
55% = yellow

Page 21
1. hollow
2. fist
3. nine ounces
4. nine
5. food

Page 24
1. T 6. T
2. T 7. F
3. F 8. F
4. F 9. T
5. T 10. T

Answer Key

Page 25
1. waste
2. lymph
3. infection
4. glands
5. white

Page 26
Across:
1. gland
3. waste
5. lymph
6. fluid

Down:
1. germs
2. blood
3. white
4. tubes

Page 27
1. kidneys
2. connect
3. filter
4. Urine
5. units

Page 28
Across:
1. abdominal
3. waste
5. nephrons
7. kidneys

Down:
2. bladder
4. urine
6. spine

Page 29
1. oxygen
2. mouth
3. windpipe
4. breathe in
5. blood
6. oxygen
7. carbon dioxide
8. food
9. breathed
10. respiration

Page 32
Across:
3. olfactory
6. nose
7. moist
9. nostrils

Down:
1. air
2. mouth
4. filters
5. odors
8. interprets

Page 35
1. ribs
2. cage
3. spinal cord

4. skull
5. 350
6. phosphorus
7. skeleton
8. 206

Page 36
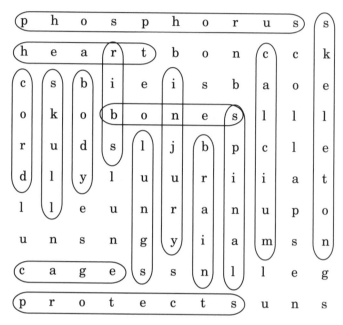

Page 37
1. The biggest bone in your body is your thighbone.
2. The smallest bone in your body is the stirrup located in your ear.
3. Blood travels through your bones in blood vessels.

Page 38
1. When you break a bone, it usually grows back as strong as it was before you broke it.
2. After you break a bone, it begins to mend immediately.
3. Bones contain calcium and other minerals.
4. The soft substance in some bones is called red marrow.
5. Red marrow makes new red blood cells.
6. Blood travels through your bones in blood vessels.
7. Answers will vary.

Fascinating Facts About The Human Body—Grades 4–6 • ©1995 The Education Center, Inc. • TEC370

Answer Key

Page 39
1. hard
2. inside
3. minerals
4. jelly
5. blood

Page 40

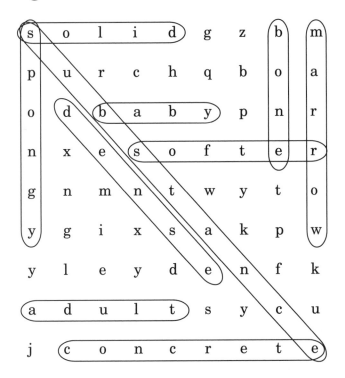

Page 41
1. b
2. c
3. c

Page 42
1. backbone/spine
2. neck or neck section
3. look at ceiling, tuck your chin next to your chest, turn your head from side to side
4. 12
5. compacts
6. sacrum
7. tailbone/coccyx

Page 44
1. The tailbone is at the very bottom of the backbone.
2. The spinal column is a stack of vertebrae.
3. Another name for the backbone is the spine or spinal column.
4. The sacroiliac is the joint that connects the sacrum and the upper vertebrae.
5. The spinal column supports the body and protects the spinal cord.

Page 46
1. cranium
2. mandible
3. scapula
4. clavicle
5. sternum
6. rib
7. humerus
8. vertebra
9. pelvis
10. ulna
11. radius
12. carpal
13. metacarpal
14. phalange
15. femurs
16. patella
17. fibula
18. tibia
19. tarsal
20. metatarsal

Page 47
1. The elbow joint acts like a hinge between the upper and lower arm bones.
2. The humerus is the upper arm bone.
3. The radius and ulna are the two bones in the lower arm.
4. Answers may vary.

Page 48
Across:
4. ligaments
6. rotate
7. ulna
8. degrees

Down:
1. hinge
2. joins
3. joint
5. together
6. radius
9. elbow

Page 49
1. T
2. F
3. T
4. T

Page 50
1. humerus
2. collarbone
3. shoulder
4. deltoid
5. three
6. degrees

Answer Key

Page 51

1. On the ends of the bones is a spongy area with space where nerves and blood vessels run in and out.
2. Less than 50% of bones are hard, 25% is water, and the rest is living cells and tissue.
3. The arm and leg bones are called the long bones.

Page 53

1. Cartilage cushions the bones and minimizes friction between them.
2. Cartilage is a soft tissue that is more slippery than ice.
3. At birth, my bones were mostly cartilage.

Page 54

Cartilage is flexible and gives when bones are jarred, so it makes a good shock absorber.

Page 55

1. shoulder—ball-and-socket
2. wrist—sliding/gliding
3. neck—pivotal
4. elbow—hinge

Page 56

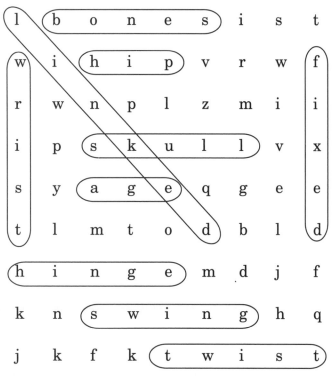

Page 58

Across:
2. calf
3. fibrous
5. tendon
6. connects
8. move

Down:
1. Achilles
4. ankle
6. cord
7. toes

Page 61

1. F
2. T
3. F
4. T
5. T
6. F
7. T
8. T
9. F
10. T

Page 63

1. b
2. b
3. c
4. c

Page 64

Across:
3. dies
4. blood
5. glucose
8. brain

Down:
1. tissue
2. complex
6. circulates
7. hungry

Page 67

1. spinal, bundle, nerves
2. cord, column
3. holes, vertebrae
4. brain, spine

Page 72

Across:
2. temperature
4. layer
5. epidermis
8. follicles
10. sun

Answer Key

Down:
1. sweat
3. water
6. dermis
7. cools
9. vessels

Page 73
1. keratin
2. protein
3. inches

Page 74
1. T   6. T
2. F   7. T
3. F   8. F
4. T   9. T
5. F   10. F

Page 78
1. middle
2. inner
3. outer
4. brain
5. nerve
6. eardrum
7. balance
8. vibrates

Page 79
1. see
2. feel
3. smell
4. hear
5. taste

Page 81
1. The digestive system processes food.
2. energy for maintenance and repair
3. mouth, esophagus, stomach, intestines

Page 82

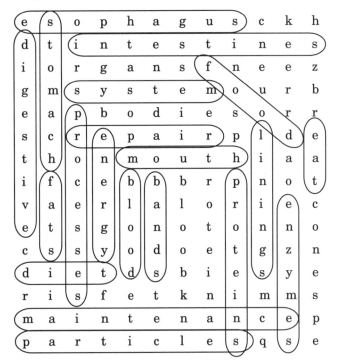

Page 83
1. F   6. F
2. T   7. T
3. T   8. F
4. T   9. T
5. F   10. T

Page 85
1. 32
2. 4
3. job

Page 87
1. crown
2. root
3. enamel
4. dentine
5. dentine
6. pulp chamber/blood vessels/nerves

Page 88
1. enamel
2. dentine
3. crown
4. pulp chamber
5. root canal

Answer Key

6. nerves and blood vessels
7. root

Page 91
1. b
2. c
3. c

Page 92
1. sugars, starches, fats, vitamins, and minerals
2. largest
3. processes
4. blood
5. cells
6. small intestine
7. complex
8. digest

Page 93
1. two
2. enzymes
3. carbohydrates, proteins, fats

Page 94
1. c   5. a
2. e   6. g
3. b   7. d
4. f

Page 95
1. F   5. F
2. T   6. F
3. T   7. F
4. F   8. F

Page 97
1. hormones
2. Insulin
3. adrenaline

Page 98
1. b
2. c
3. d
4. a

Page 99
1. ovum
2. zygote
3. 46

Page 100
1. c   6. i
2. f   7. j
3. b   8. e
4. a   9. h
5. g   10. d
Bonus: 480 eggs

Page 101
1. 46
2. 23
3. 100,000
4. 46

This is to Certify

that

_____

has completed a course in fascinating facts
about the human body!

Hip, Hip, Hooray!!!

_____
signature

_____
date

Fascinating Facts About The Human Body—Grades 4–6 • ©1995 The Education Center, Inc. • TEC370

CONGRATULATIONS!

YOU HAVE LEARNED ABOUT THE
CIRCULATORY AND LYMPHATIC SYSTEMS!

A TERRIFIC JOB BY:

_____

_____
signature

_____
date

Fascinating Facts About The Human Body—Grades 4–6 • ©1995 The Education Center, Inc. • TEC370

What A Brain!

To: _____

For: Learning about the nervous and sensory systems

_____
signature

_____
date

Fascinating Facts About The Human Body—Grades 4–6 • ©1995 The Education Center, Inc. • TEC370

ZOWIEEEEEEEEE!

_____

is an expert on the digestive system.

_____
signature

_____
date

Fascinating Facts About The Human Body—Grades 4–6 • ©1995 The Education Center, Inc. • TEC370

Hear Ye! Hear Ye!

Let it be known that

_____

is hereby declared an expert on the body's respiratory system.

_____
signature

_____
date

Fascinating Facts About The Human Body—Grades 4–6 • ©1995 The Education Center, Inc. • TEC370

Truly Stupendous!

_____

knows all about the

muscular and skeletal systems.

Congratulations

on being able to name _____ bones.

_____
signature

_____
date

Gold Medal Achievement

GOLD

_____

has completed _____ bonus activities.

_____
signature

_____
date

Fascinating Facts About The Human Body—Grades 4–6 • ©1995 The Education Center, Inc. • TEC370

Gold Medal Achievement

GOLD

_____

has completed _____ research activities.

_____
signature

_____
date

Fascinating Facts About The Human Body—Grades 4–6 • ©1995 The Education Center, Inc. • TEC370